Laboratory Manual
to accompany
Mastering A+ Certification

James L. Antonakos
Kenneth C. Mansfield Jr.
Broome Community College

Prentice
Hall

Upper Saddle River, New Jersey
Columbus, Ohio

Editor in Chief: Stephen Helba
Assistant Vice President and Publisher: Charles E. Stewart, Jr.
Product Manager: Scott Sambucci
Production Editor: Alexandrina Benedicto Wolf
Production Coordination: Custom Editorial Productions, Inc.
Design Coordinator: Diane Ernsberger
Cover Designer: Thomas Borah
Cover Image: Corbis Stock Market
Production Manager: Matthew Ottenweller

This book was set in Times Roman by Custom Editorial Productions, Inc. It was printed and bound by Courier/Kendallville. The cover was printed by Phoenix Color Corp.

Notice to the Reader: All product names listed herein are trademarks and/or registered trademarks of their respective manufacturer.

The publisher and the authors do not warrant or guarantee any of the products and/or equipment described herein, nor has the publisher or the authors made any independent analysis in connection with any of the products, equipment, or information used herein. The reader is directed to the manufacturer for any warranty or guarantee for any claim, loss, damages, costs, or expense arising out of or incurred by the reader in connection with the use or operation of the products or equipment.

The reader is expressly advised to adopt all safety precautions that might be indicated by the activities and experiments described herein. The reader assumes all risks in connection with such instructions.

All character names (e.g., Ken Koder and Joe Tekk) are property of Pearson Education. Copyright pending.

Pearson Education Ltd., *London*
Pearson Education Australia Pty. Limited, *Sydney*
Pearson Education Singapore, Pte. Ltd.
Pearson Education North Asia Ltd., *Hong Kong*
Pearson Education Canada, Ltd., *Toronto*
Pearson Educación de Mexico, S.A. de C.V.
Pearson Education—Japan, *Tokyo*
Pearson Education Malaysia, Pte. Ltd.
Pearson Education, *Upper Saddle River, New Jersey*

10 9 8 7 6 5 4 3 2 1
ISBN: 0-13-094433-5

Preface

This *Laboratory Manual to accompany Mastering A+ Certification* provides students with the hardware and software exposure to the personal computer needed to prepare for the two A+ exams. Ideally, each student should have hands-on experience with every Windows version that is available. This manual provides an opportunity to reinforce the similarities and, more importantly, to explore the differences that set the operating systems apart from each other.

Each lab activity contains an Introduction section, a multi-step Procedure section, and a Discussion and Conclusion section that poses additional questions for consideration. These lab activities support the theory presented in the companion textbook, *Mastering A+ Certification,* by James L. Antonakos and Kenneth C. Mansfield Jr.

Each student should maintain a lab journal—a notebook where everything is recorded as a lab activity is performed. This serves two purposes: 1) Information from the journal is used when writing the report for the lab activity; and 2) The journal is a good field reference when actual troubleshooting and maintenance are necessary.

The instructor may pick and choose lab activities as desired or even combine labs if necessary, as some of the activities are shorter than others. Ideally, students should work with a partner on each experiment, provide assistance to each other, and promote discussion of the lab topics. This, of course, is left to the discretion of the instructor.

With the hands-on experience gained by performing the fifty lab activities in this manual, students will face future computer situations with confidence and skill.

James L. Antonakos
antonakos_j@sunybroome.edu
http://www.sunybroome.edu/~antonakos_j

Kenneth C. Mansfield Jr.
mansfield_k@sunybroome.edu
http://www.sunybroome.edu/~mansfield_k

Contents

For Mayda Bosco,
who helps us tremendously.

Lab Activity 1
Identifying PC Components

REFERENCE

Exercise 2

INTRODUCTION

In this lab activity, we examine the components that make up a complete computer system.

PROCEDURE

1. Carefully examine the computer system assigned to you. How many of the components shown in Figure 1.1 does your system contain?
2. What components of your system are not shown in Figure 1.1?
3. What type of connectors are used for the keyboard, mouse, and printer?
4. What is the capacity of each hard drive?
5. What is the speed of the CD-ROM drive? Is it a writeable CD-ROM?
6. Is the computer connected to a network? If so, what is the type (modem, network interface card) and speed of the connection?
7. Carefully remove the cover.
8. Is the display adapter an ISA, PCI, or AGP card?
9. How many free slots are available on the motherboard?
10. Can you identify other adapter cards (modem, network interface card, etc.)?
11. Replace the cover and boot the system.
12. Right-click on **My Computer** and choose **Properties** from the pop-up menu.
13. What is the amount of RAM and the processor type shown in the General System Properties window?
14. Close the window.

DISCUSSION AND CONCLUSION

Using a word processor, write your own detailed explanations of the results and observations made during the experiment. To begin, try to say something about each step.

In addition, provide answers to the following questions:

1. How does your lab computer compare to a computer system currently available on the market?
2. What new hardware component did you learn about by looking inside the system?

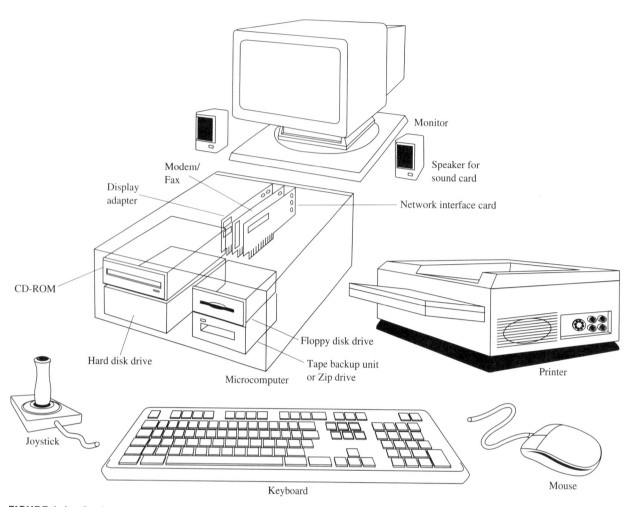

FIGURE 1.1   A microcomputer system

2

Lab Activity 2
Computer Environments

REFERENCE

Exercise 3

INTRODUCTION

In this lab activity, we examine the physical environment of the microcomputer laboratory.

PROCEDURE

1. What is the temperature of the lab? How is the temperature controlled?
2. Are the lab computers left on at all times? If not, what is the typical power-on and power-off scenario (for example, are the computers turned on in the morning and off at night)?
3. How are the computers protected from excess heat?
4. Is the computer clean (free of dust, etc.)? If not, carefully vacuum out all dust and other particles.
5. What are the sources of electrical noise in the lab? Can any of them be reduced or eliminated?
6. Are the computers connected to surge protectors?
7. Are any uninterruptible power sources used? If so, what is their capacity?
8. What precautions are available for handling ESD?
9. How many computer stations are there in the lab? Are they all equipped the same?
10. What additional equipment is available in the microcomputer lab?

DISCUSSION AND CONCLUSION

Using a word processor, write your own detailed explanations of the results and observations made during the experiment. To begin, try to say something about each step.

In addition, provide answers to the following questions:

1. Is the microcomputer lab comfortable? Is it a good place to do work? Is there anything you would change?
2. If you have a computer at home, how does its environment compare with the micro-computer lab?
3. Is there a chart showing how the lab is organized (network connections, location of specialized equipment)?

Lab Activity 3
Selecting a Boot Device

REFERENCE

Exercise 3

INTRODUCTION

In this lab activity, we investigate the various ways to boot a computer. We also create a Windows Startup disk.

PROCEDURE

1. Boot up your lab computer and enter the BIOS setup program.
2. Look for the selection item that allows you to choose your boot device.
3. Review the entire list of available boot devices. How many of the following devices are available?
   - Floppy
   - Hard drive
   - CD-ROM
   - SCSI
   - Network

   Record the current boot device settings.
4. Set up the BIOS to search for boot devices in the following order (if possible): CD-ROM, then hard disk. Place an ordinary application CD into the CD-ROM. Save the new BIOS settings and boot the computer. What message is displayed as the computer tries to boot from the CD-ROM?
5. Create a Windows Startup disk. The steps are as follows:
   - Insert a blank floppy into the disk drive.
   - Place the Windows CD into the CD-ROM.
   - Left-click on **Start**, then select **Settings** and **Control Panel**.
   - Double-click **Add/Remove Programs** and left-click the **Startup Disk** tab. You should see a display window similar to that shown in Figure 3.1.
   - Left-click the **Create Disk** button.

   When the Startup disk has been created, left-click **OK** to close the window.
6. What files have been written to the Startup disk?
7. If there is a README.TXT file on the Startup disk, open it with a word processor and read it.

FIGURE 3.1   Preparing to
create a Windows Startup disk

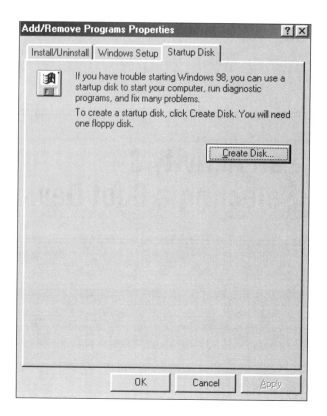

8. Shut down the computer and then reboot, again entering the BIOS setup program. Change the boot sequence to floppy, then hard disk. Save the settings and reboot.

9. Does the system boot from the floppy? What special messages are output? If a RAM-DRIVE is created, how do its contents compare to the Startup disk?

10. Remove the floppy from the disk drive and reboot the computer. Enter the BIOS setup program and restore the original boot device settings. Save them and reboot.

DISCUSSION AND CONCLUSION

Using a word processor, write your own detailed explanations of the results and observations made during the experiment. To begin, try to say something about each step.

In addition, provide answers to the following questions:

1. Why would you want a computer to boot from a network?
2. What is a Startup disk good for?

Lab Activity 4
Building a Computer from Scratch

REFERENCE

Exercise 4

INTRODUCTION

In this lab activity, we explore the steps required to build a working computer system, given all of the individual components.

PROCEDURE

1. Gather the following system components:

Hardware
- Tower or mini-tower (with power supply)
- Motherboard
- Processor
- RAM
- Floppy drive with cable
- IDE hard drive with cable
- IDE CD-ROM drive with cable
- Display adapter and video monitor
- Keyboard
- Mouse

Software
- MS-DOS install disks
- Windows CD-ROM

2. Mount the motherboard to the chassis of the tower.
3. Connect the front-panel wires for the Reset button, hard drive activity light, and speaker.
4. Attach the motherboard power connector(s).
5. Install the processor. For a ZIF socket, lift the restraining handle, insert the processor (refer to motherboard manual for proper orientation), and then reseat the handle. The processor cooling fan may mount directly on top of the processor with a flexible metal strap. Plug in the cooling fan.

    For slot 1 processors, carefully and firmly press straight down on the processor card as you insert the card into the connector.

6. Install the RAM. SIMMs and DIMMs are inserted at an angle and gently rocked into place. They should stick straight up when fully seated and also click into place on each end.
7. Slide the floppy drive into its slot and secure it with two or more screws. Connect a power cable to it. Attach both ends of the floppy drive cable between the drive and the motherboard. Refer to the motherboard manual for pin-1 orientation on the cable socket.
8. Repeat step 7 for the hard drive. Be sure the drive is jumpered for Master/Single operation. Connect the hard drive cable to the Primary Master connector on the motherboard.
9. Repeat step 8 for the CD-ROM drive.
10. Plug in the display adapter card and secure it with a screw. Connect the monitor to the adapter card and plug in the monitor.
11. Plug in the keyboard and the mouse.
12. Connect the power cord and plug it in. Turn on the computer. The BIOS should autodetect the hard drive and test the RAM. Since the hard disk has no operating system, the boot process will eventually require a system disk.
13. Insert the operating system installation media (floppy or CD-ROM). Boot the system and follow the installation instructions.
14. Be sure to make an Emergency Boot Disk when prompted.

DISCUSSION AND CONCLUSION

Using a word processor, write your own detailed explanations of the results and observations made during the experiment. To begin, try to say something about each step.

In addition, provide answers to the following questions:

1. What difficulties (if any) were encountered when assembling the hardware components?
2. Are there any steps that required additional safety or careful attention? List them.
3. Was it necessary to make sure that each of the hardware components were supported by Windows?
4. What difficulties (if any) were encountered when performing the software installation?

Lab Activity 5
Power Supply and Connectors

REFERENCE

Exercise 5

INTRODUCTION

In this lab activity, we measure power supply voltages and explore power ratings.

PROCEDURE

1. Remove the system cover so that you have access to the power supply. Boot up the system.
2. Carefully grasp a spare 4-pin power connector. Hold it so that the yellow wire is on the left and the red wire on the right, as indicated in Figure 5.1(a).

FIGURE 5.1   Various voltage connectors from the power supply

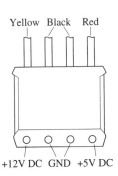

(a) Disk drive connector

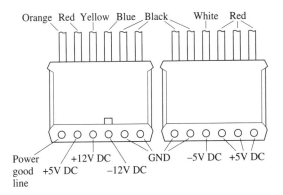

(b) Motherboard connectors

3.3V	3.3V	COM	5V	COM	5V	COM	PW-OK	5VSB	12V
1	2	3	4	5	6	7	8	9	10
11	12	13	14	15	16	17	18	19	20
3.3V	–12V	COM	PS-ON	COM	COM	COM	–5V	5V	5V

(c) ATX power connector

3. Set your digital multimeter to measure DC volts.
4. Place the black meter lead on the connector for one of the black wires and the red meter lead on the connector for the red wire. Record the voltage reading (it should be 5 volts).
5. Move the red meter lead to the yellow wire. Record the voltage reading (it should be 12 volts).
6. How many individual power cables are provided by the power supply, not including power for the motherboard?
7. Locate the manufacturer's label or nameplate on the power supply cover. What is the wattage rating of the power supply?
8. What is the maximum current available at 5 volts and 12 volts?
9. Repeat step 8 for the –5 volt and –12 volt outputs.
10. Are there 3.3 volts available from the power supply? How can you tell? Record its maximum current if available.
11. Multiply the individual voltage outputs by their respective maximum currents to find the individual power ratings. Add all the ratings together to find the total power. How does this power compare to the power rating listed on the nameplate?
12. Shut down the computer and replace the system cover.

DISCUSSION AND CONCLUSION

Using a word processor, write your own detailed explanations of the results and observations made during the experiment. To begin, try to say something about each step.

In addition, provide answers to the following questions:

1. How many different styles of power connectors did you see?
2. Is there any way to expand a single output connector into two connectors? If so, would this be safe to do?

Lab Activity 6
Identifying Motherboard ICs

REFERENCE

Exercises 6, 7, 8, and 10

INTRODUCTION

In this lab activity, we familiarize ourselves with all of the integrated circuits used to make a functional motherboard.

PROCEDURE

1. If possible, obtain a copy of the manual for the motherboard in your lab computer. Otherwise, locate the model number of your motherboard and search the Web for information on it. Try www.motherboards.org.
2. Give your motherboard a good visual inspection. Spend several minutes looking over the entire board. Locate all the integrated circuits, look at the different connector styles, read all the words and identifiers silk-screened onto the motherboard, and note the various jumpers.
3. Attempt to locate all of the following integrated circuits:
   Processor
   External cache
   System RAM
   BIOS ROM
   PCI-to-host bridge
   PCI-to-ISA bridge
   CMOS/clock
   Integrated peripheral controller (COM, LPT, etc.)

   There may be several styles of integrated circuits used on the motherboard. These include surface mount and through-hole integrated circuits. Bridge integrated circuits will have many pins (possibly coming out of all four sides) and be larger than other integrated circuits. You should write down the part number of any integrated circuit with more than 14 pins. In the absence of a motherboard manual, search the Web for the part numbers to identify the integrated circuits.

   Look for the cache and PCI-to-host bridge to be close to the processor. Look for the PCI-to-ISA bridge to be close to the ISA sockets. The BIOS ROM should be close to the ISA connectors, also.

FIGURE 6.1 Device Manager display indicating bridge IC part numbers

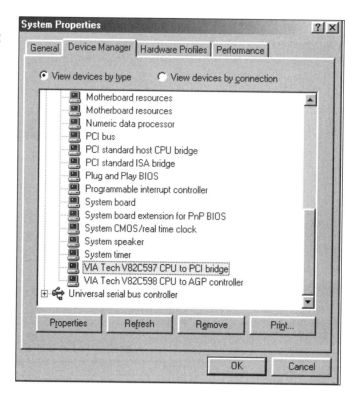

4. Windows may help identify some ICs for you. Right-click on **My Computer** and choose **Properties** from the pop-up menu. Then left-click on **Device Manager**.
5. Double-click **System devices** to view the entries for each hardware device. As indicated in Figure 6.1, there may be entries for the bridge ICs, as well as others.
6. Figure 6.2 shows the block diagram of a typical motherboard. Add the part numbers of the ICs you identified to the figure and make any other necessary changes.

DISCUSSION AND CONCLUSION

Using a word processor, write your own detailed explanations of the results and observations made during the experiment. To begin, try to say something about each step.

In addition, provide answers to the following questions:

1. Imagine that one IC could contain everything necessary for the operation of a motherboard (processor, RAM, peripheral and bus controllers). Estimate how many pins would be required to interface the IC with ISA, PCI, and AGP connectors, as well as IDE, COM, LPT, mouse, and keyboard signals. What would be the advantages and disadvantages of having such an IC?
2. Why do you imagine that driver files are required to operate the motherboard electronics?

**FIGURE 6.2 Typical
motherboard block diagram**

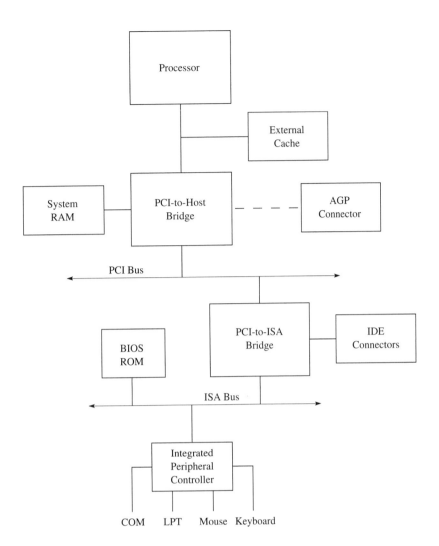

Lab Activity 7
Inserting/Removing Motherboard ICs

Exercise 8, Appendix E

In this lab activity, we practice removing and inserting ICs on the motherboard. Typically, the ICs you would normally use to do this are the processor (to upgrade it), external cache (to add more), RAM (to add more), a coprocessor, and the BIOS ROM.

Be sure to observe all safety and anti-static precautions when working with motherboard components.

1. Remove the cover of your lab computer to expose the motherboard. It may be necessary to unplug some of the ribbon cables to get better access to the ICs on the motherboard.
2. The BIOS ROM and cache ICs may be DIPs. If so, carefully remove them by pulling straight up with an IC removal tool or by gently rocking each end up slightly with a flatblade screwdriver. Be sure to note the position of pin 1 on the IC before you re-move it.
3. Carefully reinsert each DIP by inserting all the pins on one side into the socket, then gently aligning all pins on the opposite side and pushing straight down. If a pin bends during insertion, remove the IC and use needlenose pliers to straighten the pin.
4. Remove a system RAM SIMM or DIMM by pushing the metal locking tabs away from each side and rocking the SIMM or DIMM forward at an angle. Then slide the SIMM or DIMM up out of the socket.
5. Reinsert the memory chip by sliding it into the socket at an angle, carefully lining up the connector pads on the chip with the socket. Rock the SIMM or DIMM gently into an upright position. If the chip is aligned correctly, it will snap into place. Do not force the chip upright or push down on it hard to seat it.
6. If the motherboard contains a socket for a coprocessor, it may be a DIP socket, or a PLCC or PGA socket. PLCC and PGA ICs are inserted into their sockets with a great deal of force. Unless you have the proper tools, do not attempt to remove a socketed PLCC or PGA IC.

7. If the processor is mounted on a ZIF socket, it is a simple matter to remove the CPU. Just unlatch the handle and lift it up to remove pressure on the IC pins. Then lift the processor out of the ZIF socket. You may need to remove the processor fan first. There should be a thin metal bar across the fan that is latched on one side. Unlatch the bar and remove the fan. Note the orientation of the CPU before removing it from the ZIF socket.

8. What is the socket number on the ZIF socket (as in Socket 7)?

9. Pentium II/III processors come mounted on a card with their own built-in fans. The card plugs into a Slot 1 connector. Card guides on each side of the connector contain latches that snap into place to keep the card secure. Unlatch them before trying to pull the card out of the connector.

10. Reinsert the CPU card into the Slot 1 connector and latch it into place.

11. Reconnect any ribbon cables removed in step 1 and replace the system cover.

DISCUSSION AND CONCLUSION

Using a word processor, write your own detailed explanations of the results and observations made during the experiment. To begin, try to say something about each step.

In addition, provide answers to the following questions:

1. What difficulty did you have when working with the motherboard ICs?
2. Which sockets allow you to reinsert an item incorrectly (pin 1 not in the correct position)?

Lab Activity 8
Motherboard Configuration

REFERENCE

Exercises 6 through 14

INTRODUCTION

In this lab activity, we take a detailed look at the adjustments that can be made to a typical motherboard and its various properties. This is useful to understand, especially when replacing a motherboard or upgrading a processor.

PROCEDURE

1. If possible, obtain a copy of the manual for the motherboard in your lab computer. Otherwise, locate the model number of your motherboard and search the Web for information on it. Try www.motherboards.org.
2. Look for the following settings and their associated motherboard jumpers. What are they set to?
   - Clear CMOS RAM
   - DIMM clock selection
   - CPU voltage selection
   - CPU speed selection
   - CPU bus frequency ratio
3. What other jumper options are available on your motherboard?
4. What processors are supported by the motherboard? What type of CPU socket is used?
5. List all the wires and cables plugged into the motherboard (speaker, reset button, etc.).
6. What is the maximum RAM that may be installed? The maximum cache? Is it possible to flash program the BIOS ROM?
7. Record the information printed on top of each major IC on the motherboard. Using the motherboard manual (or the Internet), identify each IC (BIOS ROM, PCI bridge, integrated peripheral controller, etc.).
8. Boot up the lab computer. Right-click on **My Computer** and choose **Properties** from the pop-up menu.
9. Left-click on **Device Manager**. Double-click **System devices** and locate the **Motherboard resources** entries. Double-click each one to see what resources are in use. Figure 8.1 shows some reserved memory resources (the address range of the BIOS ROM). What range of memory is reserved by your motherboard? What I/O ports?

FIGURE 8.1 Motherboard memory resources

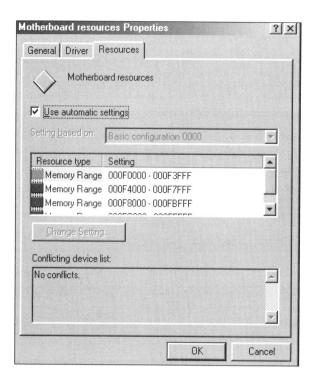

10. Spend some time examining the other entries in the System devices category. At a minimum, record the settings for the following devices:
    - Numeric data processor
    - DMA controller
    - Programmable interrupt controller
    - System board
    - CMOS/clock
    - PCI bridges
    - System speaker
    - System timer

DISCUSSION AND CONCLUSION

Using a word processor, write your own detailed explanations of the results and observations made during the experiment. To begin, try to say something about each step.

In addition, provide answers to the following questions:

1. What enhancements can be performed on your motherboard? Is there room for more system RAM or cache? Is there a faster processor available?
2. How can the characteristics of a motherboard be changed without making any hardware modifications?

Lab Activity 9
Examining Interrupt and
I/O Port Settings

REFERENCE

Exercise 9

INTRODUCTION

In this lab activity, we examine two important system resources: interrupts and input/output (I/O) ports. Incorrectly assigned interrupt or I/O settings can cause a device, or even the entire system, to not function properly.

PROCEDURE

1. If you have the DEBUG utility on your system, open up a DOS window and enter this command: **DEBUG > INTS.TXT**.
   This will cause the output from the DEBUG program to be sent to the file INTS.TXT.
2. After pressing **Enter**, you will not see any output on the screen, even when you enter the following DEBUG command: **D0:0 L 400**.
   This command instructs DEBUG to display 1024 bytes of memory beginning at offset 0 in segment 0, which is where the interrupt vector table resides. After pressing **Enter**, you will not see any of the memory data displayed on the screen. It is all being redirected to the INTS.TXT output file.
3. Now type **Q** and press **Enter** to quit DEBUG.
4. Open the INTS.TXT file with a word processor and print out a copy of it.
5. Navigate to your system's interrupt display. This is done by right-clicking on **My Computer** and selecting **Properties** to bring up the System Properties window. Then left-click on **Device Manager**, left-click **Computer**, and choose **Properties**. Your window will be similar to that shown in Figure 9.1.
6. Record all 16 interrupt assignments.
7. Returning to the Device Manager window, left-click the **Radio** button for **input/output (I/O)**. You should see a display similar to Figure 9.2.
8. Record the input/output port assignments for the following devices:
   - DMA controller
   - Programmable interrupt controller
   - System timer
   - Keyboard
   - Real-time clock
   - Speaker
   - Numeric data processor

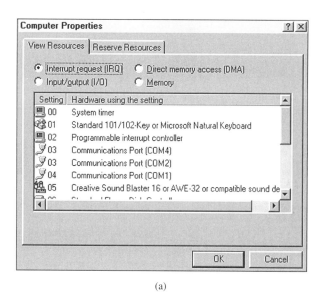

(a)

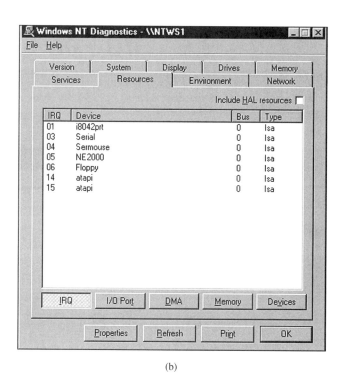

(b)

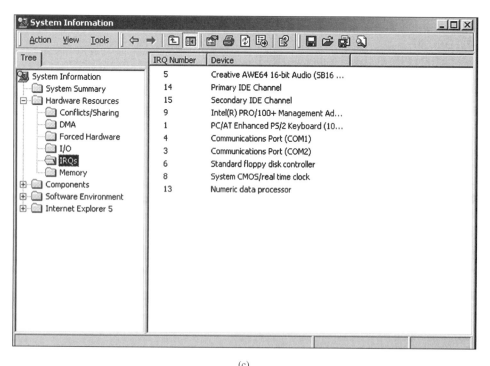

(c)

FIGURE 9.1   (a) Interrupt assignments in Windows 95/98, (b) Windows NT IRQ Resources, and (c) Windows 2000 IRQ display

FIGURE 9.2 Input/output port assignments

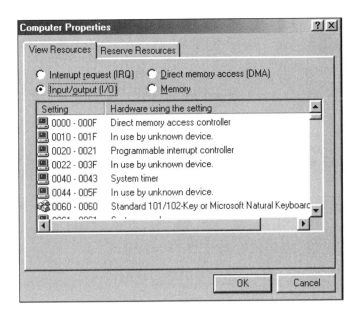

- Sound card
- Network card
- COM1
- COM2
- Floppy controller
- IDE controller
- PCI controller
- Video adapter
- LPT1

9. What other devices do you find I/O assignments for?

10. To check the interrupt and I/O assignments (as well as other resources) for a specific device, you can also go directly to the device in the Device Manager window and double-click it. Then left-click the **Resources** tab. You will see a display similar to that in Figure 9.3.

11. Record the interrupt and I/O settings for four different devices.

FIGURE 9.3 Resources used by a sound card

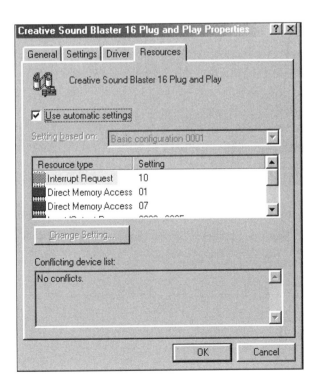

Using a word processor, write your own detailed explanations of the results and observations made during the experiment. To begin, try to say something about each step.

In addition, provide answers to the following questions:

1. Are any interrupt vectors set to 0000:0000?
2. Are there multiple interrupt vectors that all contain the same addresses?
3. Why not use a single interrupt for all devices?
4. Why not use a small handful of I/O ports for all devices?

Lab Activity 10
Memory: Chips and Management

REFERENCE

Exercise 10

INTRODUCTION

In this lab activity, we explore the use of the MEM program to report memory allocation, monitor memory usage on a running system, and remove/insert memory chips into their motherboard sockets.

PROCEDURE

The first part of this lab activity gives you the opportunity to have your computer system use as much of its memory as possible. The second half has you examine the location and type of RAM used by the system.

1. Use the following DOS command to check how memory is used in your computer. If you have a printer available, redirect the output to the printer:

   ```
   C> MEM /P
   ```

2. From step 1, determine whether your system has *extended* or *expanded* memory and how much. If you have problems with this, check with your instructor.
3. In this step, you force DOS to use as much higher memory as possible. Using a text editor, add the following DOS commands to your CONFIG.SYS file:

   > DEVICE = [drive][path]HIMEM.SYS
   > DOS   = HIGH
   > DEVICE = [drive][path]EMM386.EXE

4. Now reboot your system. Again, run the DOS memory program:

   ```
   C> MEM /P
   ```

   What differences do you now see in the memory allocation of your system?
5. If your system has a device driver, such as a mouse, you can use DOS to try to force the driver into high memory. Modify your CONFIG.SYS file to add the following:

   > DOS = HIGH, UMB
   > DEVICEHIGH = [path and name of device]

6. Again, reboot your system. Using the DOS memory program

```
C> MEM /P
```

determine what difference there is now in the allocation of your system memory.

7. If your system has a TSR program, attempt to force as much of it as possible into high memory. Add the following to your AUTOEXEC.BAT file:

LOADHIGH [program name]

8. Again, reboot your system. Using the DOS memory program

```
C> MEM /P
```

determine what difference there is now in the allocation of your system memory.

9. To use as much extended memory as possible, install a virtual disk in high memory. To do so, make sure the program VDISK.SYS (for IBM DOS) or RAMDRIVE.SYS (for MS-DOS) is on your DOS disk. Then add the following command, as appropriate to CONFIG.SYS:

(IBM DOS) DEVICE = VDISK.SYS /E
(MS-DOS) DEVICE = RAMDRIVE.SYS /E

10. Again, reboot the system and verify that the virtual disk has been installed. Use the DOS memory program

```
C> MEM /P
```

Determine what difference there is now in the allocation of your system memory.
11. Shut down the system and remove the cover.
12. Locate the system RAM. What type is it (DIMM, SIMM) and how many are there? Are there any free RAM sockets?
13. Record all the information printed on the RAM.
14. Carefully remove one of the RAMs and reinsert it. Note that there may be springy metal clips on the sides of the RAM socket that hold the RAM chip in place. Also, insert the RAM at an angle and then rock it into an upright position. If the connector pins are not seated correctly, the RAM chip will not snap into place once it is upright.
15. Replace the cover and boot up the system.
16. Left-click on **Start**, then select **Programs**, **Accessories**, **System Tools**, and finally **System Monitor**.
17. If necessary, use the **Edit**, **Remove Item** pull-down menu to make room for some charts in the System Monitor window. Then use **Edit**, **Add Item** to add Memory Manager selections. View the results for 10 minutes as you open and close other applications and generally use the system.
18. Close the System Monitor application.

DISCUSSION AND CONCLUSION

Using a word processor, write your own detailed explanations of the results and observations made during the experiment. To begin, try to say something about each step.

In addition, provide answers to the following questions:

1. How useful is the information provided by the MEM program?
2. Can you determine the size (in MB) of each RAM chip in your system? For example, if you have two SIMMs and a total of 64 MB of system RAM, then each SIMM stores 32 MB.
3. What did you find interesting about watching the charts in the System Monitor window?

Lab Activity 11
Identifying Motherboard
Expansion Connectors

REFERENCE

Exercise 11

INTRODUCTION

In this lab activity, we examine the various types of expansion connectors. These include ISA, PCI, and AGP connectors, as well as others.

PROCEDURE

Note: Be sure to protect exposed components from static electricity.

1. Follow the appropriate procedures to remove the cover of your lab computer so that the motherboard is clearly visible.
2. Count the number of black ISA connectors.
3. If there are ISA adapter cards plugged into the ISA connectors, what are the functions of each card? Carefully remove each card and examine it. Look at the components mounted on the adapter card. Study the metal pads on the connectors. Is the connector keyed (notched between two pins)? Are there any markings or lettering on the motherboard by each connector?
4. Repeat steps 2 and 3 for the white PCI connectors.
5. Scan the motherboard for the PCI-to-ISA bridge integrated circuit. Record the part numbers and other markings off of each large integrated circuit on the motherboard. Use the Web to look up the part numbers to discover the bridge.
6. Carefully examine the brown AGP connector and its associated graphics adapter.
7. What other expansion connectors are located on the motherboard?
8. Reassemble the computer and boot it up to make sure that everything is working properly. Then shut down the computer and reboot it. Enter the system BIOS setup program. Examine the menu entries for Chipsets, or PCI/PNP, and record the different PCI and AGP variables and their settings.
9. Open **Device Manager** (left-click **Start**, **Settings**, **Control Panel**, and **System**). Figure 11.1 shows a sample Device Manager display.
10. Examine the PCI and AGP entries in the System devices section. Either double-click the desired device, or left-click it and select **Properties**. Note the associated interrupts, I/O port addresses, and memory addresses used by each device. Figure 11.2 shows a sample of the information provided in System devices.
11. Close the Control Panel windows.

FIGURE 11.1 System devices categories

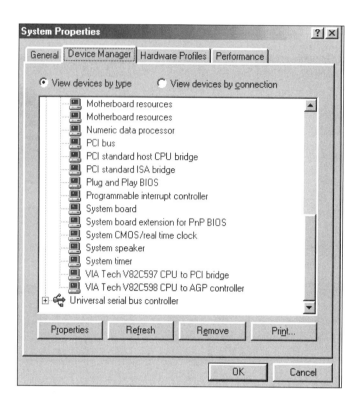

FIGURE 11.2 Some of the input/output ports associated with the PCI bus

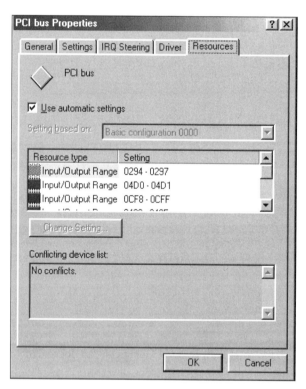

Using a word processor, write your own detailed explanations of the results and observations made during the experiment. To begin, try to say something about each step.

In addition, provide answers to the following questions:

1. Is it possible to plug a PCI or AGP adapter card into its socket backwards?
2. Are the components on ISA, PCI, and AGP adapter cards on one side or both sides of the circuit board?
3. Which connectors are closest to the processor? Which are the farthest away?

Lab Activity 12
Working with the System BIOS

REFERENCE

Exercise 13

INTRODUCTION

In this lab activity, we take a detailed look at the many items controlled by BIOS settings. Information provided by the BIOS ID is also examined. Since it is easy to introduce problems into your system with incorrect BIOS settings, we will not change any settings to see their results.

PROCEDURE

1. Boot your lab computer and record the BIOS ID number from the startup screen. Try pressing the Pause key to freeze the screen and provide time to copy down the BIOS ID.
2. Use the BIOS ID to identify the chipset used on the motherboard and the motherboard manufacturer.
3. Reboot again if necessary and enter the BIOS setup program.
4. Record all of the categories on the BIOS menu.
5. Examine all of the BIOS settings in all categories. In particular, look for these items and record their settings and values:
   - Boot sequence
   - Cache settings
   - Typematic settings
   - Video BIOS shadow
   - DRAM settings
   - CPU/System temperature
   - CPU fan speed
   - Power supply voltages
   - Power management settings
   - Plug-and-Play/PCI settings
   - AGP settings
   - Peripheral settings (COM ports, LPT)
6. Search the Web for the manufacturer of your BIOS and determine if there is an upgrade for it. If so, do you need to replace the BIOS chip or can you flash it?

7. In the hard drive category, examine the different types of hard drives preloaded into BIOS. How many are there?
8. Exit BIOS setup without saving any changes and shut down the computer.
9. If allowed by your instructor, carefully remove the BIOS chip from the motherboard and reboot the computer. Does it boot?
10. Leave the chip out for 15 minutes. Then reinsert it into its socket and reboot the computer. Check the system time and date. Is it correct, behind by 15 minutes, or totally incorrect?

DISCUSSION AND CONCLUSION

Using a word processor, write your own detailed explanations of the results and observations made during the experiment. To begin, try to say something about each step.

In addition, provide answers to the following questions:

1. Why is it useful to identify the motherboard manufacturer in the BIOS ID?
2. The security feature on BIOS provides password-based access. Why would it be necessary to protect BIOS with a password?

Lab Activity 13
Handling POST Errors

REFERENCE

Exercise 12

INTRODUCTION

In this lab activity, we create and observe several POST errors.

PROCEDURE

Observe and record the following error codes. Make sure you listen for audible error codes as well as look for numerical error codes.

1. Boot a normally working computer. Observe all beeps, the duration (short or long) of the beeps, and how many beeps there are. At the same time, view your screen to observe all numerical values produced by your computer's POST. Record this information.
2. Turn off the computer and remove the keyboard plug from the computer so that the keyboard is no longer attached to the computer. Now reboot the computer. Again, record all of your POST observations.
3. Turn off the computer and reconnect the keyboard. Now, while rebooting the computer, hold down a key on the keyboard (this simulates a stuck key). Record your observations (including the key you held down).
4. Turn off the computer. Remove the monitor cable from the computer case so that the monitor is no longer connected to the computer. Reboot the system and record your observations of the POST.
5. Carefully remove the video adapter card and reboot the computer. Record the POST beep codes.
6. Plug the video adapter back in, connect the monitor, and reboot the computer. The system should boot normally.
7. Shut down the computer and remove the system RAM. Reboot and record the POST error codes.
8. Shut down the computer and reinstall the system RAM.
9. Disconnect power to the floppy disk (or the hard disk). Reboot and record the POST error code.
10. Reconnect power to the disk drive and then carefully remove the processor. Reboot the computer. What POST error codes, if any, are produced? What do you see on the screen?
11. Power down, reinsert the processor, and reboot to make sure the system is back to normal.

DISCUSSION AND CONCLUSION

Using a word processor, write your own detailed explanations of the results and observations made during the experiment. To begin, try to say something about each step.

In addition, provide answers to the following questions:

1. Suppose you attempt to boot a computer and there are no audible codes produced. The system does not boot either. In fact, the BIOS program does not even run. What are the possible problems?
2. Explain why just getting a beep code is actually a good sign.
3. How many combinations of four long or short beeps are there?

Lab Activity 14
Adding/Replacing a Hard Drive

REFERENCE

Exercises 16 and 18

INTRODUCTION

In this lab activity, we look at several hard drive scenarios that commonly occur when adding or replacing a hard drive. Preparing the newly installed hard disk for use by the operating system requires partitioning and formatting, both of which are covered in Lab Activity 16.

PROCEDURE

ADDING A SINGLE/MASTER HARD DRIVE

1. Set the jumpers on the new drive for Master/Single operation.
2. Connect the IDE ribbon cable to the drive. Note the colored stripe on the cable indicating pin 1. Look closely at the connector on the drive to locate its pin-1 side as well. Plug the other end of the cable into the Primary Master IDE connector on the motherboard.
3. Attach power to the new drive.
4. Boot the computer with a floppy containing MS-DOS or use a Windows startup disk (go to **Add/Remove Programs** to make a startup disk). If the BIOS is new enough, it will autodetect the new drive. Otherwise, you must enter the BIOS setup program and detect the drive or enter the disk geometry values.
5. Run FDISK to partition the new drive as indicated in Lab Activity 16.
6. Run FORMAT to format the logical drive as indicated in Lab Activity 16. The drive must be formatted as a System disk so that you can boot from it. To install Windows on the new drive, add the required CONFIG.SYS and AUTOEXEC.BAT statements to support a CD-ROM drive. Then run the SETUP program from the CD-ROM.

ADDING A SLAVE HARD DRIVE

1. Set the jumpers on the new drive for Slave operation.
2. Connect the IDE ribbon cable to the drive. Note the colored stripe on the cable indicating pin 1. Look closely at the connector on the drive to locate its pin-1 side as well.

Plug the other end of the cable into the Primary Slave IDE connector on the mother-board. Alternately, you could connect the new drive to the same ribbon cable used for the Master drive if there are two connectors on one end of the ribbon cable.

3. Attach power to the new drive.
4. Boot the computer. If the BIOS is new enough, it may autodetect the new drive. Otherwise, you must enter the BIOS setup program and detect the drive or enter the disk geometry values.
5. Run FDISK to partition the new drive as indicated in Lab Activity 16.
6. Run FORMAT to format the logical drive as indicated in Lab Activity 16. The drive should be formatted as a non-System disk since it is a slave and will not contain the operating system files.

REPLACING A HARD DRIVE

1. Back up the existing hard drive.
2. Add the second hard drive as a slave, as in the previous scenario.
3. Use the backup of the original drive to place a copy of all files onto the new drive. Alternately, after adding the slave, use an application like PartitionMagic to copy the partition from the original drive to the slave.
4. Shut down the computer and remove the original drive.
5. Change the jumper settings on the new drive to Master/Single and reboot the computer. Adjust BIOS parameters as necessary.

DISCUSSION AND CONCLUSION

Using a word processor, write your own detailed explanations of the results and observations made during the experiment. To begin, try to say something about each step.

In addition, provide answers to the following questions:

1. Why must there be a Master and a Slave in a two-drive system?
2. Why not leave the old hard drive in a system alone when adding a new hard drive and skip the transfer of all the files from the old drive to the new drive? What is the advantage of putting the old files on a new drive?

Lab Activity 15
Hard Drive Backup

REFERENCE   Exercise 17

INTRODUCTION   In this lab activity, we practice backing up and restoring files on the hard drive.

PROCEDURE   To do this activity, you will use the A: drive as the target drive (the drive that will contain the backed-up files) and the C: drive as the source drive (the drive that contains the files to be backed up).

1. Make sure the target disk is formatted.
2. Change the volume name of the source disk to **SOURCE** and the volume name of the target disk to **TARGET**.
3. Clearly label the target disk as TARGET.
4. On the C: disk, create the directory and file structure shown in Figure 15.1 or work with a directory specified by your instructor.
5. Place the target disk in drive A:. Make drive C: the active drive.
6. Make the MYSTUFF directory the active directory.
7. You will now back up all the files and subdirectories on the source disk to the target disk. From the source drive (with MYSTUFF as the active directory), enter

   C:> BACKUP C: A: /L/S

8. After the backup process is completed, look at the directory of the target disk and record what you see (include the volume name as well as the names of the files).
9. Try to erase the files on the target disk by using the DOS ERASE command. Record the message you get on the screen when you try this.
10. Use the DOS ATTRIB command to check the attributes of the files on the target disk. Record what you observe.
11. Go to the root directory of the C: disk. Observe the new file there called BACKUP.LOG. Using the DOS TYPE command, observe and record the contents of this file.
12. Repeat this process using PKZIP and PKUNZIP, and/or WINZIP.

FIGURE 15.1 Directory and file structure for C: disk.

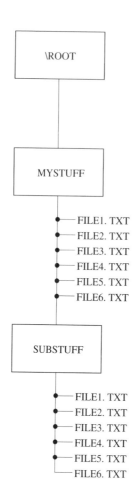

13. If there is a writeable CD-ROM drive in the lab, your instructor will demonstrate backing up files to a CD-ROM. Note that over 600 MB of data can be backed up to a single CD-ROM.
14. Repeat step 13 for a tape backup unit. Compare the time required to back up the same amount of data between the tape backup and the CD-ROM.

DISCUSSION AND CONCLUSION

Using a word processor, write your own detailed explanations of the results and observations made during the experiment. To begin, try to say something about each step.

In addition, provide answers to the following questions:

1. What message appeared on the screen just before the backup process when you first backed up the source disk with the BACKUP C: A: /L /S command? Explain why this message was there.
2. Did the volume name of the target disk change after the backup process was completed? If so, why do you think this happened?
3. Explain how a 600-MB CD-ROM backup may actually contain over one gigabyte of data.

Lab Activity 16
Hard Drive Partitioning
and Formatting

REFERENCE

Exercises 16 and 18

INTRODUCTION

In this lab activity, we utilize the FDISK and FORMAT utilities to partition and format a new or existing hard drive. These procedures must be performed before an operating system may be installed or to use the drive for storage of files.

The operations performed in this exercise are potentially damaging to existing files, so enter each command with caution. Only a few of the many different partitioning scenarios are explored. You are encouraged, with the proper precautions, to experiment with other FDISK and FORMAT situations.

PROCEDURE

VIEWING PARTITION INFORMATION USING FDISK

1. Boot up your lab computer and open a DOS window.
2. Enter **FDISK** at the command prompt and press **Enter**.
3. If FDISK determines that your drive is larger than 512 MB, it may ask you if you want to enable support for large drives. The default answer of Yes is acceptable, so press **Enter** again.
4. You should now see the FDISK Options menu, as indicated in Figure 16.1.
5. Enter **4** to display the partition information for the current disk and press the **Enter** key.
6. Record the partition information for all partitions shown. This includes the following:
   • Drive letter
   • Status
   • Type
   • Volume label
   • Size (in MB)
   • File system
   • Percentage of total disk size
7. Press **Esc** to return to the main menu.
8. If your system has a second hard disk, select option 5.

**FIGURE 16.1   Windows 98
FDISK utility**

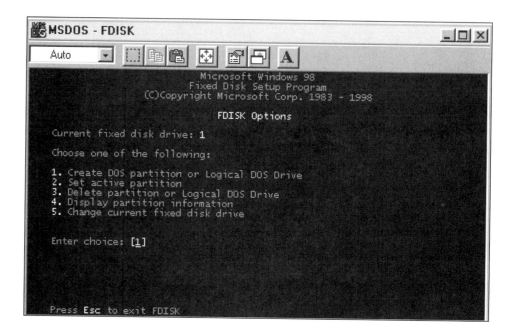

9. Enter **2** to select the second hard disk and press **Enter**.
10. Repeat steps 5 through 7 for this hard disk.
11. Press **Esc** at the main menu to exit to DOS.
12. Double-click on **My Computer**.
13. Right-click on the icon for drive **C:** and select **Properties** from the pop-up menu.
14. Compare the partition information provided by Windows with that given by FDISK. Record the partition information.
15. Repeat steps 13 and 14 for all other partitions.

CREATING A PARTITION

1. Start up FDISK and select a drive with at least 10 MB of free space.
2. To create a DOS partition, enter **1** at the main menu and press **Enter**.
3. Enter **2** to create an extended DOS partition and press **Enter**.
4. FDISK will display the free space on the disk and allow you to enter the size of the new partition in MB or in percentage. Type in **10** if there is at least 10 MB of free space. Otherwise, type in a number that is half of the available free space.
5. FDISK will display the new partition along with the original partitions. The file system will be UNKNOWN. Press **Esc** to continue.
6. FDISK will now have you set up a logical drive in the new partition. Enter **5** for the size (in MB) of the logical drive and press **Enter**.
7. FDISK will display the logical drive information. Press **Esc** to return to the main menu.
8. Press **Esc** again to exit FDISK. It will warn you that the computer must reboot to enable the new partition. *Warning:* This may cause other drive letters (including CD-ROM drives) to change. Other errors may show up during reboot as well due to the drive letter changes. Later in this experiment, the same partition is deleted, which will restore the original drive letters after rebooting.

FORMATTING A PARTITION

1. Open a DOS window.
2. Select the partition you wish to format. *Note:* All data on the partition will be lost. This is not a problem with a new partition, but an existing partition should be backed up if necessary.

3. To format the partition, enter the FORMAT command followed by the drive letter and colon, as in **FORMAT E:**, and press **Enter**.
4. FORMAT will warn you that all data on the partition will be lost. Enter **Y** to proceed with the format and press **Enter**.
5. The formatting will take place, followed by a request for the volume label. Type in **NEWDRIVE** and press **Enter**.
6. FORMAT will display the formatting information and exit.
7. Double-click **My Computer** to verify that the NEWDRIVE disk drive is available.
8. Copy files to the NEWDRIVE partition, install an application on it, or access it in some other way to verify that it operates properly.

DELETING A PARTITION

1. Open a DOS window and start up the FDISK program.
2. Enter **3** to delete a partition or logical drive and press **Enter**.
3. FDISK will ask for the drive to delete. Type in **E** and press **Enter**.
4. FDISK will now ask for the volume label. Enter the volume label of the E: drive and press **Enter**.
5. FDISK will ask you if you are sure. Enter **Y** and press **Enter**.
6. FDISK will delete the drive. Press **Esc** to continue.
7. FDISK will warn you that drive letters may have changed. Press **Esc** to return to the main menu.
8. Press **Esc** again to exit FDISK. It will force you to reboot to reorganize the drives.
9. Double-click on **My Computer** after rebooting to verify that the drive letters are back to normal.

DISCUSSION AND CONCLUSION

Using a word processor, write your own detailed explanations of the results and observations made during the experiment. To begin, try to say something about each step.

In addition, provide answers to the following questions:

1. Explain how partitioning allows a single physical hard drive to operate like multiple drives.
2. FDISK does not allow you to copy a partition (although other applications, such as Partition Magic, do). Explain why this would be helpful.
3. Why should you use caution when working with partitions?

Lab Activity 17
Video Adapter/Monitor Operation

REFERENCE

Exercise 19

INTRODUCTION

In this lab activity, we investigate the operation of the video monitor and display adapter.

PROCEDURE

1. What is the model number of the monitor connected to your lab computer? Who is the manufacturer?
2. Does the monitor contain a CRT or is it a flat-panel display?
3. Does the monitor conform to EPA Energy Star requirements?
4. Boot up the computer so that the desktop is displayed. Experiment with the monitor's video controls. Change the horizontal size and position of the display. Do the same for the vertical controls. This may require you to learn how to use the built-in menu of monitor controls.
5. Shut down the system and remove the cover.
6. What type of display adapter does the computer use (PCI, AGP, embedded on motherboard)?
7. Carefully remove the display adapter, if possible. Give the card a good visual.
8. What is the video chipset used by the display adapter?
9. To check the display adapter resources, right-click on **My Computer** and choose **Properties** from the pop-up menu. Then left-click the **Device Manager** tab.
10. Double-click on **Display adapters**.
11. Double-click on the entry for your display adapter. Then left-click the **Resources** tab. The Resources window should look similar to that shown in Figure 17.1.
12. Record the interrupt, I/O port, and memory settings for the display adapter.
13. If there is a **Diagnostics** tab, left-click it and run all diagnostics available for the display adapter. Then examine the remaining properties windows.
14. Return to Device Manager and double-click **Monitors**. Does the name of your monitor show up?
15. Examine the Monitor properties.

FIGURE 17.1 Video adapter resources

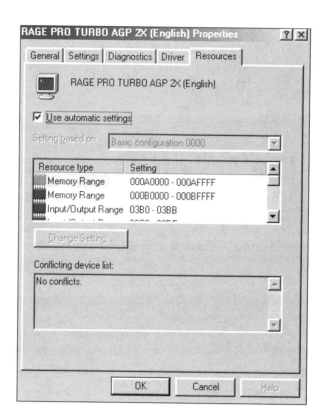

RAGE PRO TURBO AGP 2X (English) Properties

General | Settings | Diagnostics | Driver | Resources

RAGE PRO TURBO AGP 2X (English)

☑ Use automatic settings

Setting based on: Basic configuration 0000

Resource type	Setting
Memory Range	000A0000 - 000AFFFF
Memory Range	000B0000 - 000BFFFF
Input/Output Range	03B0 - 03BB

Change Setting...

Conflicting device list:

No conflicts.

OK   Cancel   Help

DISCUSSION AND CONCLUSION

Using a word processor, write your own detailed explanations of the results and observations made during the experiment. To begin, try to say something about each step.

In addition, provide answers to the following questions:

1. How difficult was it to learn how to use the monitor's video controls?
2. How does Windows discover the name of the monitor connected to the computer?

Lab Activity 18
Keyboard and Mice Operation

REFERENCE

Exercise 21

INTRODUCTION

In this lab activity, we explore the various features and characteristics of the keyboard and mouse.

PROCEDURE

1. Open up the Keyboard Properties window by left-clicking **Start**, **Settings**, **Control Panel**, and **Keyboard**. Figure 18.1 shows the Speed properties window.

FIGURE 18.1   Keyboard speed settings

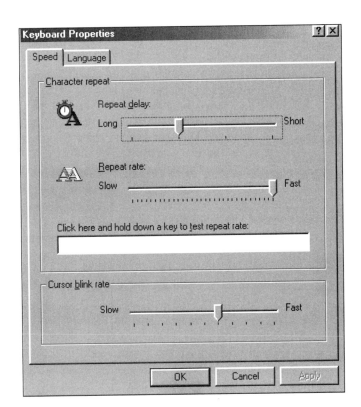

FIGURE 18.2   Initial Mouse Properties window

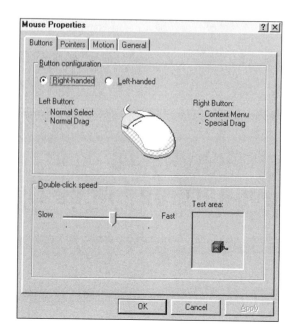

2. Adjust the Repeat delay and rate. How does this affect your ability to use the keyboard?
3. Vary the blink rate of the cursor from slowest to fastest and estimate the blink rate (blinks/second).
4. Left-click on the **Language** tab and record the keyboard language(s) installed.
5. Cancel out of the Keyboard Properties window.
6. Shut down the computer and disconnect the keyboard cable. Reboot the computer. What error message, if any, is reported by BIOS and/or Windows?
7. Examine the keyboard connector. What type is it (USB, 5-pin, proprietary)?
8. Shut down the computer and re-attach the keyboard cable. Reboot the computer to verify the keyboard is functioning.
9. Open up the Mouse Properties window by left-clicking **Start**, **Settings**, **Control Panel**, and **Mouse**. Figure 18.2 shows the Buttons properties window.
10. Vary the double-click speed from slowest to fastest. What rate is comfortable for you?
11. One by one, examine the adjustable features found under the **Pointers**, **Motion**, and **General** tabs.
12. Turn the mouse over and carefully twist off the cover holding the rubber-coated ball. Remove the ball and examine the inside of the mouse. Are the moving parts clean? Is there any fuzz or lint wrapped around any of the rollers? Replace the ball and cover.
13. Cancel out of the Mouse Properties window.
14. Shut down the computer and disconnect the mouse cable. Reboot the computer. What error message, if any, is reported by BIOS and/or Windows?
15. Examine the mouse connector. What type is it (USB, 9-pin, proprietary)?
16. Shut down the computer and re-attach the mouse cable. Reboot the computer to verify that the mouse is functioning.

DISCUSSION AND CONCLUSION

Using a word processor, write your own detailed explanations of the results and observations made during the experiment. To begin, try to say something about each step.

In addition, provide answers to the following questions:

1. Why would someone want more than one language installed on a keyboard?
2. What are the user-friendly aspects of the keyboard and mouse? How can a user customize the keyboard and mouse?
3. Why make the double-click speed of the mouse adjustable? Explain why one speed may not be good for everyone.

Lab Activity 19
Working with Printers

REFERENCE

Exercise 20

INTRODUCTION

In this lab activity, we examine the printer hardware characteristics and the help provided by Windows when a printing problem occurs. Additional work with the printer is provided in Lab Activity 38, Using a Network Printer.

PROCEDURE

1. What type of printer is connected to your lab computer or available in the lab as a networked printer (dot-matrix, laser, ink-jet, etc.)?
2. If the printer is a network printer, is it hosted by a computer or is it a stand-alone network printer? What is its name on the network?
3. What type of cable connects to the printer? Describe the connector used at each end of the cable.
4. Test the printer by printing a test page. Left-click on **Start**, and then choose **Printers** from the Settings submenu.
5. Right-click on the desired printer and choose **Properties** from the pop-up menu. Left-click the **Print Test Page** button on the printer's properties display window.
6. Even if the test page printed perfectly, Windows will ask you if the page printed correctly. Select **No** to open up the printer troubleshooter.
7. The troubleshooter will prompt you to perform certain tasks, then ask you if they fixed the problem. Always answer **No** so that the troubleshooter has to keep working. Eventually, you will get to the end of the troubleshooting suggestions provided by Windows Help. How many things did Windows have you do to try to fix the problem?
8. Return to the desktop. Disconnect the printer cable and try to print another test page. What error is reported by Windows, if any?
9. Reconnect the printer cable.
10. To check the printer port hardware settings, right-click on **My Computer** and choose **Properties** from the pop-up menu. Then left-click on the **Device Manager** tab.
11. Double-click the **Ports (COM & LPT)** entry.
12. Double-click the **Printer Port** entry and left-click the **Resources** tab. You should see a display window similar to that shown in Figure 19.1.

FIGURE 19.1   Printer port resources

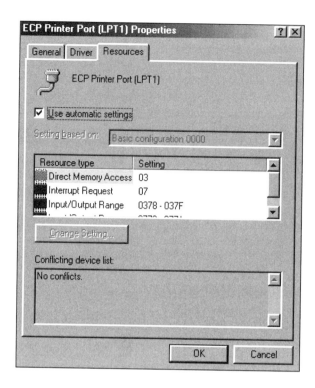

13. Record the resource settings (interrupt, I/O ports, etc.) for the printer port.
14. Return to the desktop.
15. Examine all of the printers in the lab. Which ones need cleaning or other servicing? Make a list for your instructor.

DISCUSSION AND CONCLUSION

Using a word processor, write your own detailed explanations of the results and observations made during the experiment. To begin, try to say something about each step.

In addition, provide answers to the following questions:

1. Does the Windows printer troubleshooter do a good job?
2. Locate the prices for several types of printers: laser, color ink-jet, network-based, etc.

Lab Activity 20
Using MODEMs and Network
Interface Cards

REFERENCE Exercises 22 and 25

INTRODUCTION In this lab activity, we familiarize ourselves with the operation of MODEMs and network interface cards, the two gateways to the world of networking.

PROCEDURE

MODEM

1. Read the documentation that accompanies the modem used by your system.
2. If one is not already present, create a text file on your disk that can be sent from one computer to another over the telephone modem.
3. If it has not already been done, properly connect your computer to a designated telephone outlet.
4. Your instructor will assign a telephone number for you to dial. Using your modem software, dial the assigned number and set parameters to an agreed-to setting.
5. Transmit the text file on your disk to the remote station.
6. Hang up and then verify (by telephone) that your text file has been received.
7. Now set your modem software so that your computer is in the receive mode. An assigned remote terminal will now contact you and send you a text file. Make sure that the received text file is stored on your floppy disk.
8. By telephone, verify to the sender that the text file has been properly received.
9. Experiment with the AT commands. Use the reference provided with your modem or find additional AT command information on the Web.

NETWORK INTERFACE CARD

1. Use a crossover UTP cable to directly connect two computers through their network interface cards. For computers without a network interface card, install a NIC using the following instructions as a guide:
   • Remove computer cover.
   • Locate open expansion slot and install the network interface card.

- Boot the computer and install software according to the manufacturer instructions. Depending on the NIC manufacturer, you may be asked to supply the Windows installation CD-ROM, a manufacturer CD-ROM, or a floppy disk. *Note:* Several reboots may be necessary to complete the hardware installation.
- If the network interface card is not recognized by the operating system, it may be necessary to choose the correct software adapter driver from the list of supported manufacturers or from the CD-ROM or floppy disk that accompanies most network interface cards. *Note:* The Windows operating system provides additional help via the network troubleshooter.
- After the card has been installed properly, replace the computer cover.
- Verify that the NetBEUI and TCP/IP protocols are installed by reviewing the Network settings in the Control Panel. If one or both of these protocols are not listed, select the **Add** option, then select **Protocols** and pick them from the list of Microsoft protocols. Obtain proper settings information from your instructor or the network administrator.

2. Enable file sharing on each machine. This is done as follows:
   - Right-click on **Network Neighborhood**.
   - Select **Properties**.
   - Left-click on **File and Print Sharing**.
   - Check the box that allows file sharing.
   - Left-click on **OK**.
3. Now share the C: drive on each machine. This is done as follows:
   - Left double-click on **My Computer**.
   - Right-click on the drive **C:** icon.
   - Select **Sharing** from the pop-up menu.
   - Select the **Shared As** option.
   - Left click on **OK**.
4. Left double-click on **Network Neighborhood**. Does each machine see the other one? *Note:* It may take several seconds for any changes to be reflected in the Network Neighborhood. You should click the **Refresh** option in the **View** pull-down menu frequently to guarantee that you have an accurate view of the network. Note how long it takes for the changes to occur.
5. If each Network Interface Card has a BNC connector, disconnect the UTP cable and attach a T-connector to the NIC. On one side of the T-connector, attach one end of a coaxial cable. On the other side, attach a 50-ohm terminator. Are the machines still visible in Network Neighborhood? Again, allow some time for the changes to be reflected in the Network Neighborhood.
6. Remove one of the 50-ohm terminators.
7. Are the machines still visible in Network Neighborhood?
8. Open up WINIPCFG and examine its properties. This is done by left-clicking **Start** and choosing the **Run** option. Then enter **WINIPCFG** and left-click **OK**. Record the adapter address (6-byte hexadecimal number) and any IP addresses indicated.

DISCUSSION AND CONCLUSION

Using a word processor, write your own detailed explanations of the results and observations made during the experiment. To begin, try to say something about each step.

In addition, provide answers to the following questions:

1. What difficulties, if any, did you encounter when using the modem?
2. What Windows diagnostics are available for the modem? Go to the **Modem** entry in Device Manager to investigate.
3. What difficulties, if any, did you encounter when installing the network interface card?
4. What kinds of problems are caused by the removal of a 50-ohm terminator?

Lab Activity 21
Using the CD-ROM, Sound Card, and Multimedia Devices

REFERENCE

Exercises 23 and 24

INTRODUCTION

In this lab activity, we take a look at the features and properties of the CD-ROM drive and sound card, as well as typical multimedia devices.

PROCEDURE

CD-ROM

1. Boot up your lab computer.
2. Right-click on **My Computer** and select **Properties** from the pop-up menu. Left-click the **Device Manager** tab.
3. Double-click the **CDROM** entry. Then double-click a CD-ROM drive from the list to view its properties.
4. Left-click the **Settings** tab. You should see a window similar to that shown in Figure 21.1.
5. If there is a small boxed question mark in the upper right corner, left-click it, then move the mouse pointer over one of the text items in the window and left-click again. What information is displayed when you do this?
6. Use the question mark to get information on the other items in the window.
7. Close the window.
8. Put an audio CD into the CD-ROM drive. Does it play? Does a CD-player application open up?
9. Remove the audio CD and insert an application CD.
10. Does the application or setup program on the CD start automatically? If not, can you determine why not?
11. Cancel the setup program and eject the application CD.
12. What statements, if any, do CONFIG.SYS and AUTOEXEC.BAT contain that relate to the CD-ROM drive?

SOUND CARD

1. Boot up your lab computer.
2. Right-click on **My Computer** and select **Properties** from the pop-up menu. Left-click the **Device Manager** tab.

FIGURE 21.1   CD-ROM settings

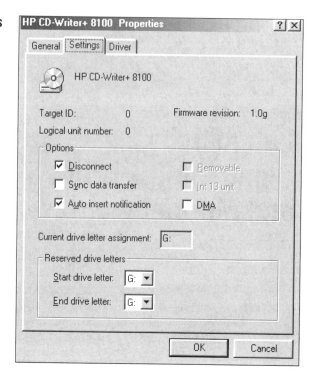

3. Double-click the **Sound, video and game controllers** entry. Then double-click your sound card from the list to view its properties.
4. Left-click the **Resources** tab. Record the interrupt, I/O port, and DMA settings.
5. Close the Device Manager window. Left-click on **Start**, then choose **Programs**, **Accessories** and **Entertainment**. Then left-click on **Sound Recorder**.
6. Left-click on **File** and select **Open** from the pull-down menu. In your Windows directory, there will be several WAV files, such as CHIMES.WAV and DING.WAV. Open a WAV file and play it. What is the sound-length of the file? How many bytes are stored in the file? What is the data rate in bytes/sec during play?
7. Repeat step 6 for three other WAV files of different lengths.
8. Close the Sound Recorder.
9. What statements, if any, do CONFIG.SYS and AUTOEXEC.BAT contain that relate to the sound card?

MULTIMEDIA DEVICES

1. If there is a video camera connected to your lab computer, answer the following:
   • How does the camera connect to the computer (USB, LPT port, etc.)?
   • Is the camera black and white or color?
   • What software is required to operate the camera?
   • Does system performance degrade when the camera is being used?
   • What are the camera's properties in Device Manager?
2. If there is a scanner connected to your lab computer, scan two or more images and compare the size of each image file created by the scanner software. Also, answer the following:
   • How does the scanner connect to the computer?
   • Does the scanner software perform OCR on a scanned document?
   • What are the scanner's properties in Device Manager?
3. What other multimedia devices does your lab computer contain?

GENERAL

1. Shut down the computer and remove the system cover.
2. Is there an audio cable connecting the CD-ROM drive to the sound card or motherboard?
3. If the audio cable plugs into the motherboard, does the motherboard contain an embedded sound chip?
4. What are the jumper settings on the CD-ROM drive?
5. If possible, remove the sound card and give it a good visual. Write down the part numbers of the integrated circuits. How many connectors are on the card and what type are they?
6. Reinstall the sound card and replace the system cover.

DISCUSSION AND CONCLUSION

Using a word processor, write your own detailed explanations of the results and observations made during the experiment. To begin, try to say something about each step.

In addition, provide answers to the following questions:

1. Why do CD-ROM drives allow a range of drive letters to be reserved?
2. What would you do if the sound card does not generate any sound?
3. What multimedia device would be useful in the lab?

Lab Activity 22
Adding Hardware

REFERENCE

Exercise 36

INTRODUCTION

In this lab activity, we examine the various details associated with the installation of new hardware. *Note:* It is important to record all BIOS, IRQ, DMA, and other settings prior to any hardware installation so that problems with the installation will not affect your ability to return the system to its previous state.

PROCEDURE

WINDOWS 95/98

1. Start the Add New Hardware wizard by left-clicking on **Start**, **Settings**, and **Control Panel**, then double-clicking on the **Add New Hardware** icon.
2. Left-click on **Next**. Windows will want to search for new Plug-and-Play hardware. Click on **Next** again to start the search.
3. No matter what hardware may be discovered by Windows, select **No, the device isn't in the list** and left-click **Next**.
4. Select **No, I want to select hardware from a list** and left-click **Next**. A list of hardware types similar to that shown in Figure 22.1 will appear.
5. Make a list of all the hardware types shown in the list. Then select a hardware type, such as **System Devices**, and left-click **Next**.
6. Examine the list of manufacturers and the models for each manufacturer.
7. Repeat steps 5 and 6 for three other hardware types, such as **Display adapters, Hard disk controllers**, or **Modem**.
8. Left-click **Cancel** to abort the installation process.
9. Your instructor may provide hardware for you to install. Keep these points in mind as you proceed:
   - Read the manufacturer's installation manual carefully before proceeding.
   - Unless the new hardware is a USB or PCMCIA device, be sure that the system is properly shut down and powered off (with the power cable unplugged).
   - During installation of the associated driver files, Windows may discover a newer version of a file already on the system. It is best to keep the newer version rather than overwriting it with an older copy from the installation media.

FIGURE 22.1   Choosing a
hardware device to add

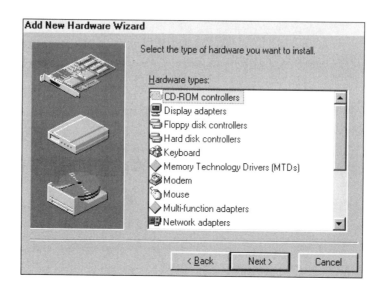

- You may be required to reboot several times before the new hardware finally works.
- Plug-and-Play hardware may not be automatically detected.

WINDOWS NT SERVER

1. Insert the Windows NT Server CD-ROM and navigate to the **Drvlib** folder. The contents should be similar to that shown in Figure 22.2.
2. Examine the contents of each hardware folder. Note the different hardware platforms available such as Alpha, i386, and Ppc.
3. Exit the folder browser.
4. Your instructor may provide hardware for you to install. Follow all manufacturer directions carefully, and remember that it may be possible to recover from a bad installation by selecting the Last Known Good configuration at boot time. Be sure to have an Emergency Repair Disk available.

FIGURE 22.2   Drvlib folder

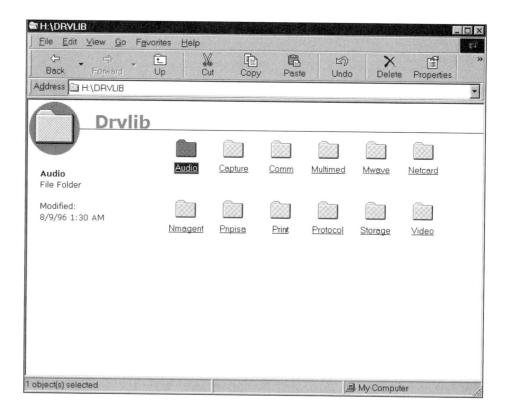

WINDOWS 2000 SERVER

1. In a manner similar to Windows 95/98, new hardware is installed in the Windows 2000 Server through the Add New Hardware wizard found in the Control Panel. Once there, select **Add/Troubleshoot a device** and left-click **Next**.
2. The Windows 2000 Server will then search for new Plug-and-Play hardware, present a list of hardware devices found, and then provide options to search for new hardware or select it from a list. Examine the list of supported hardware and note the manufacturers and models listed. Cancel the installation process when you have finished.
3. Your instructor may provide hardware for you to install. As indicated in step 9 of the Windows 95/98 section, follow all manufacturer instructions and perform all work under the supervision of your instructor.

DISCUSSION AND CONCLUSION

Using a word processor, write your own detailed explanations of the results and observations made during the experiment. To begin, try to say something about each step.

In addition, provide answers to the following questions:

1. How many different manufacturers did you discover when performing step 6 of the Windows 95/98 procedure?
2. How many different hardware platforms are supported under Windows NT Server?
3. Do your own research and discover the similarities or differences encountered when installing hardware in Windows NT Workstation and/or Windows 2000 Professional.
4. Do all versions of Windows support USB? What about Plug-and-Play?

Lab Activity 23
Getting System Information

REFERENCE

Exercises 9, 13, and 39

INTRODUCTION

In this lab activity, we use the MSINFO32 utility to obtain detailed information about the hardware in a computer system.

PROCEDURE

1. Boot up your lab computer.
2. To start the MSINFO32 utility, left-click on **Start** and choose **Run** from the Start menu. Enter **MSINFO32** in the Run window and press **Enter**.
3. After MSINFO32 opens, double-click the **Hardware Resources** entry.
4. Examine each category in the Hardware Resources list. Figure 23.1 shows an example of the first category, Conflicts/Sharing.

FIGURE 23.1   IRQ conflicts and sharing display

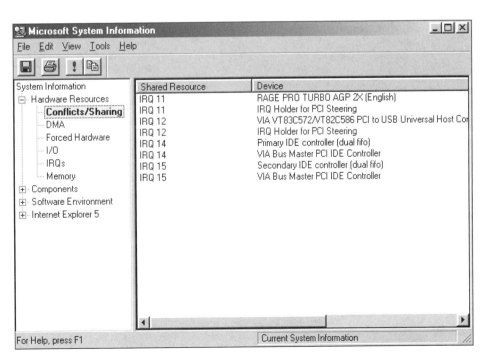

5. Examine all the categories in the Components list as well.

6. Left-click on the **File** and select **Save** from the pull-down menu. The default extension (file type) should be shown as NFO. Enter **MYSYS** as the name of the information file to be saved.

7. Close MSINFO32 and open NOTEPAD by left-clicking **Start**, selecting **Programs**, **Accessories**, and left-clicking on **NOTEPAD**.

8. Can you make sense of the information in the MYSYS file? If not, what then is the purpose of the file? Use the Help feature of MSINFO32 to find the answer to the question.

9. Open MSINFO32 again and this time save the information file as a TXT (text) file. This is done by selecting **Export** in the File menu. Enter **MYSYS.TXT** as the file name.

10. Use NOTEPAD to view the MYSYS.TXT file. Is it readable now? What information does it contain?

11. Print out a copy of MYSYS.TXT, close all applications, and shut down the system.

DISCUSSION AND CONCLUSION

Using a word processor, write your own detailed explanations of the results and observations made during the experiment. To begin, try to say something about each step.

In addition, provide answers to the following questions:

1. If your system does not have MSINFO32, is that a good enough reason to upgrade your operating system?

2. What value would the MYSYS.TXT file have to someone troubleshooting your computer? Would there be any value in e-mailing the file to a service technician?

Lab Activity 24
Adjusting the System Performance

REFERENCE

Exercise 39

INTRODUCTION

In this lab activity, we experiment with several parameters that affect the performance of the computer.

PROCEDURE

1. Boot up the lab computer. Open the System Properties window by right-clicking on **My Computer** and selecting **Properties** from the pop-up menu.
2. Left-click on the **Performance** tab. You should see a window similar to that shown in Figure 24.1.
3. Record the amount of free system resources. Close the window by left-clicking **OK**.
4. Open several applications, such as Word, PowerPoint, Excel, and Internet Explorer.
5. Reopen the Performance window. What are the free resources now? One at a time, open an additional application and view the changes to the free system resources. You will have to close and then reopen the Performance window each time. You may notice Windows getting sluggish as more applications are opened.
6. Close the Performance window and all applications opened in step 4.
7. Reopen the Performance window. What are the free resources now?
8. Was there any hard drive activity when all the applications in steps 4 and 5 were opened, aside from the initial hard drive activity when the application was first started?
9. If there was hard drive activity, does it get worse if additional applications are opened?
10. Left-click on the **Virtual Memory** button.
11. Left-click the **Radio** button for *Let me specify my own virtual memory settings* and left-click the check box for *Disable virtual memory*.
12. Left-click **OK** and reboot the computer. Record how long it takes to boot up with no further hard drive activity.
13. Set the virtual memory settings back to *Let Windows manage my virtual memory settings*.
14. Reboot the computer and record the time to finishing booting. Does it take less time with virtual memory enabled?

FIGURE 24.1 Windows performance information

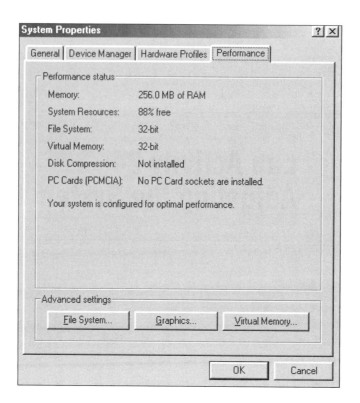

15. Reboot the computer and enter the BIOS setup program. Locate the settings for DRAM Timing and set them to slow or add the maximum number of wait states allowed by BIOS. Disable the Cache if possible. Be sure to record the original settings.
16. Save the BIOS settings and reboot. Record how long it takes to finish booting. Does it take longer than before?
17. Reboot, enter the BIOS setup program, and adjust the settings back to their original value. Save them and reboot.
18. Examine the **File System** and **Graphics** settings in the Performance window. Typically, you would not have any reason to tamper with their values (or the Virtual Memory settings), but it is good to see what can be adjusted in the event that there is a problem.

DISCUSSION AND CONCLUSION

Using a word processor, write your own detailed explanations of the results and observations made during the experiment. To begin, try to say something about each step.

In addition, provide answers to the following questions:

1. At what level of free system resources does Windows seem to be sluggish?
2. One user wanted to see what would happen when the Graphics settings were changed from Full Hardware acceleration to None. The results were surprising: a Windows protection error during reboot. After entering Safe Mode and changing the settings back, the next reboot indicated an error with the display. So, the user used Device Manager to delete the video adapter card and rebooted. Windows found new hardware (the deleted video adapter), reinstalled the drivers, and the system was back to normal. Does this scenario affect how you feel about adjusting system settings yourself?

Lab Activity 25
Networking Hardware

REFERENCE

Exercise 25

INTRODUCTION

In this lab activity, we survey the numerous hardware components associated with computer networks.

PROCEDURE

1. During a tour of a networked computer lab, look for the following networking hardware:
   - Network interface cards
   - Cabling (UTP, coax, fiber)
   - Hubs, switches, and/or routers
   - Transceivers
   - Patch panels

   Record the number of items, the manufacturers, and other information provided by labels on each item.
2. What other networking hardware is utilized? For example, are there any stand-alone network printers or print servers, Internet sharing devices, or wireless base stations?
3. Draw a diagram of the network topology in the lab.
4. What is the speed of the network? Does each user have access to the same speed?
5. Is the Internet reachable from the lab network? How did you discover this?
6. Using the proper tool and supplies, crimp an RJ-45 connector onto the stripped and prepared end of a Category 5 twisted pair cable. To prepare the end of the cable, do the following:
   a. Remove one inch of outer insulation from a suitable length (10-ft. minimum) of UTP cable. This will expose the four twisted pairs.
   b. Untwist the four pairs and straighten out the wires as much as possible.
   c. Hold the exposed wires up to the RJ-45 connector. Note the length of the wire that will be inserted into the connector. Cut off the excess length so that all eight wires are the same length.
   d. Arrange the wires in the color-coded order indicated in Table 25.1.
   e. Holding all eight wires in the proper order between your thumb and finger, slide the wires into their grooves in the connector. If the wires are the correct length, they

TABLE 25.1 RJ-45 pin assignments (568B standard)

Pin	Color	Function	Used for 10baseT
1	White/Orange	T2	✔
2	Orange/White	R2	✔
3	White/Green	T3	✔
4	Blue/White	R1	
5	White/Blue	T1	
6	Green/White	R3	✔
7	White/Brown	T4	
8	Brown/White	R4	

will go all the way to the end of their groove, with the outer cable insulation snugly inserted into the end of the connector.

    f. Insert the connector into the crimping tool and apply pressure to crimp the cable and connector together.

7. Have a lab partner attach a connector to the other end of the cable.
8. Remove an existing UTP cable connecting a computer to the lab network. Replace it with your newly crimped cable. Is the network available on the computer now?
9. Replace the original cable and submit your cable to your instructor.
10. Determine who is responsible for maintaining the networking hardware in the lab.

DISCUSSION AND CONCLUSION

Using a word processor, write your own detailed explanations of the results and observations made during the experiment. To begin, try to say something about each step.

In addition, provide answers to the following questions:

1. How old is the network equipment in the computer lab?
2. What new networking hardware would be useful in the lab?

Lab Activity 26
Logging On and Off
a Windows Computer

REFERENCE

Exercise 49

INTRODUCTION

In this lab activity, we examine the process of logging on and off a Windows computer system. *Note:* Depending on the network settings, either a name and password or a name, password, and domain will be required.

PROCEDURE

1. Perform a cold boot procedure by applying power to the computer system.
2. After the boot is complete, determine the state of the system. It may be at a login screen waiting for the user to supply necessary information or the system may be displaying the desktop. The illustrations in Figure 26.1 show the logon screen for a Windows computer.
3. Note the initial system state.
4. If your system did not ask for a password, left-click on the **Start** button and select the **Shutdown** option. Select the **Logoff** option and left-click the **OK** button.
5. If only a name and password are required, enter **APLUS** for the User name field and **TESTING** for the password field. *Note:* If a user name, password, and domain are

FIGURE 26.1   (a) Windows 95/98 logon screen

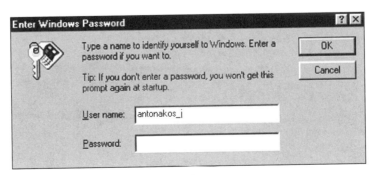

(a)

(continued on the next page)

FIGURE 26.1 *(continued)*
(b) Windows Professional login window

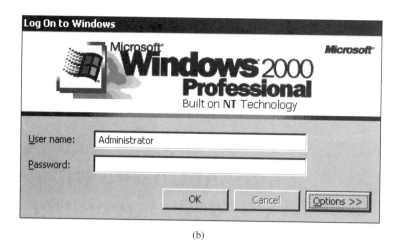

(b)

required, obtain this information from your instructor or system administrator. Enter the information supplied in the User name, Password, and Domain prompts.

6. Press the **OK** button to validate the password and perform the logon process. The Windows desktop will be displayed after a successful system logon.

7. Log off the computer system. Select **Logoff** from the Start menu if it is available, or select the **Shutdown** option and specify Logoff from the shutdown menu.

8. Repeat steps 5 and 6 using a made-up user name and password (and domain, if required) and press the **OK** button. Note any messages that are displayed by the system.

9. Press the **Caps Lock** key on the keyboard.

10. Log on using a valid user name, password, and domain information.

11. Turn off the Caps Lock feature by pressing the **Caps Lock** key again.

DISCUSSION AND CONCLUSION

Using a word processor, write your own detailed explanations of the results and observations made during the experiment. To begin, try to say something about each step.

In addition, provide answers to the following questions:

1. Does the use of upper and lower case characters make a difference when logging in to a Windows computer?

2. Does the computer system indicate a different message when the user name is correct and the password is incorrect?

3. If a domain name is required, note the messages displayed if the user name and password are correct, but the domain is incorrect.

Lab Activity 27
Getting Help in Windows

REFERENCE

Exercise 27

INTRODUCTION

In this lab activity, we examine the Help system available in Windows. In general, there are two types of help available: system and application. The system help is available directly from the Start menu or context-sensitive window, while application help is accessed through the help pull-down menu.

It is always a good idea to review all system and application help information to become familiar with all of the available features. This allows for the most efficient use of the computer systems and installed programs.

PROCEDURE

SYSTEM HELP

1. Left-click or select the **HELP** option from the Start menu to display the system help window as shown in Figure 27.1.
2. Select the **Search** tab.
3. Enter **sharing a hard disk** in the search field.
4. Record the number of topics returned.
5. Review each of the topics listed to verify that they actually contain information about sharing a hard disk. Record your results.
6. Enter **disk sharing** in the search field.
7. Record the number of topics returned.
8. Review each of the new topics listed to verify that they are relevant. Record your results.
9. Check any **Related Topics** to review all of the information available.
10. Try several other searches to see if the help system can provide better or increased access to relevant information. Record your results.

CONTEXT-SENSITIVE HELP

1. Right-click on an empty part of the desktop. Note the contents of the context-sensitive help menu.

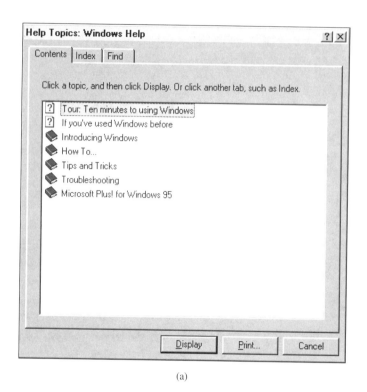

(a)

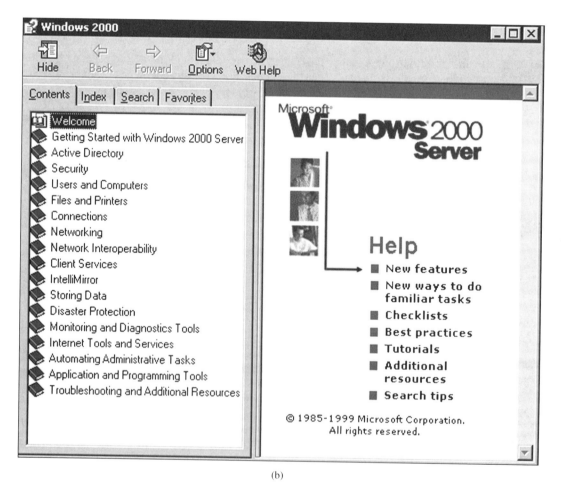

(b)

FIGURE 27.1   (a) Help Topics window and (b) Windows 2000 Server help display

2. Right-click on an icon on the desktop. Note the contents of the context-sensitive help menu.
3. Right-click on the taskbar. Note the contents of the context-sensitive help menu.

APPLICATION HELP

1. From the Start menu, run **Windows Explorer**.
2. Select **Help** from the pull-down menu.
3. Review the contents of Windows Explorer Help.
4. Close the Windows Explorer Help window.
5. Repeat steps 1 through 4 for three other Windows applications.

DISCUSSION AND CONCLUSION

Using a word processor, write your own detailed explanations of the results and observations made during the experiment. To begin, try to say something about each step.

In addition, provide answers to the following questions:

1. How many different ways can the help information be accessed?
2. Does the application help window resemble the system help window?
3. What is the advantage of providing context-sensitive help?

Lab Activity 28
Running in Safe Mode

REFERENCE

Appendix I

INTRODUCTION

In this lab activity, we examine the process of entering Safe Mode. Safe Mode is used to diagnose problems with Windows that prevent the computer from booting normally. In Safe Mode, Windows loads only a base set of drivers which will work with any type of hardware. Using Safe Mode, it is possible to correct problems that prevent Windows from booting.

PROCEDURE

1. Boot (or reboot) the computer system.
2. After the Power-On Self Test (POST), press and hold one of the shift keys or the **F5** key to enter Safe Mode. You may see a message indicating that "Windows is bypassing your startup settings." This is an indication that Safe Mode is starting.
3. Note the Safe Mode text shown on the display background as shown in Figure 28.1. Review the contents of the desktop and Start menu. Record any other changes that you notice.
4. Select **Shutdown** from the Start menu and select the **Reboot** option to automatically reboot the computer system.
5. After the POST beep, press and hold the **F8** key to select the startup mode which provides a menu for the following options on a Windows 98 system:
   - Normal
   - Logged
   - Safe Mode
   - Step-by-step configuration
   - Command prompt only
   - Safe Mode command prompt only

   If your menu is different, note the Windows operating system version and the contents of the menu.
6. From the Windows 98 menu, simply enter **3** to begin the Safe Mode boot process.
7. Reboot the computer system and test the other startup options from the menu. Record your observations.

FIGURE 28.1 Windows Safe Mode important information

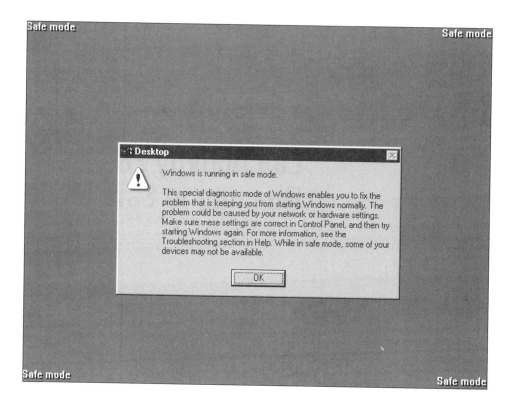

Safe mode   Safe mode

Desktop

Windows is running in safe mode.

This special diagnostic mode of Windows enables you to fix the problem that is keeping you from starting Windows normally. The problem could be caused by your network or hardware settings. Make sure these settings are correct in Control Panel, and then try starting Windows again. For more information, see the Troubleshooting section in Help. While in safe mode, some of your devices may not be available.

OK

Safe mode   Safe mode

DISCUSSION AND CONCLUSION

Using a word processor, write your own detailed explanations of the results and observations made during the experiment. To begin, try to say something about each step.

In addition, provide answers to the following questions:

1. What is the importance of Safe Mode?
2. What methods were you able to use to enter Safe Mode?
3. What is the advantage of using the menu to enter Safe Mode?
4. Does it take a longer or shorter time to display the command prompt as opposed to the Windows Safe Mode display?
5. Examine the contents of BOOTLOG.TXT. Note the significance of the information provided in the file.

Lab Activity 29
Working with the Start Menu

REFERENCE

Exercise 29

INTRODUCTION

In this lab activity, we examine the Start menu, one of the most important areas of the Windows operating system. The Start menu is automatically maintained by Windows and updated during the process of installing the operating system and application software. Windows provides for a method to add, delete, and rearrange the contents as necessary. In the next lab activity, you will explore these features on the taskbar.

PROCEDURE

EXAMINING THE CONTENTS OF THE START MENU

1. Left-click on the **Start** button. Note any differences between Figure 29.1 and your Start menu.
2. Left-click on the **Programs** folder. Note the contents.

FIGURE 29.1 (a) Windows 95 Start menu and (b) Windows 2000 Start menu

(a)

(b)

3. Left-click on the **Documents** folder. Note the contents.
4. Left-click on the **Settings** option. Note the contents.
5. Left-click on the **Search** (or **Find**, depending on the version of Windows) option. Note the contents.
6. Left-click on the **Help** option.
7. Using the **Search** tab, look for help on the Start menu. Note the result.
8. Left-click on the **Run** option.
9. Press the **Browse** button.
10. Locate and left-click on **explorer** in the list of file names.
11. Press the **Open** button to return to the Run window.
12. Select **OK** to run the explorer application. Note the result.
13. Close the explorer application program.
14. Select the **Shutdown** option. Note the shutdown options that are available.
15. Press the **Cancel** button to return to Windows.
16. Make a note of and explore any remaining Start menu options.

EXAMINING THE START MENU PROPERTIES

1. Right-click on the **Start** menu button. Note the items in the context-sensitive window.
2. Select the **Open** option from the list.
3. Right-click on the **Programs** icon.
4. Select the **Properties** option from the menu. Note the result.
5. Close the **Properties** window.
6. Double-click on the **Programs** icon.
7. Compare the display to the Programs folder in the Start menu.
8. Examine the remaining items in the Start Menu window.
9. Close the Start Menu window.
10. Right-click on the **Start** menu button.
11. Select the **Explore** menu option.
12. Scroll up in the pane displayed on the left hand side of the Windows Explorer window and note the name of the folder that contains the Start menu.
13. Review the properties for each of the entries in the Start menu and compare to the results recorded earlier.

CUSTOMIZING THE START MENU

1. Click the **Advanced** tab on the Taskbar Properties window to display a window similar to the window shown in Figure 29.2.
2. Compare the contents of the window on your system with the window shown in Figure 29.2. Note any differences.
3. Click the **Add** button.
4. Select the **Browse** option.
5. Double-click the **Program Files** folder on the C: drive.
6. Double-click the **Accessories** folder.
7. Double-click on the **Wordpad** application program (or left-click on the **Wordpad** application program and pick **Open**).
8. Note the contents of the Command Line text box.
9. Select the **Next** button to select the program folder.
10. Select **Next** to add Wordpad to the Programs folder.
11. Select **Finish** to complete the add procedure using the name Wordpad.
12. Open the **Start** menu to verify that Wordpad has been added to the Programs menu.
13. Click the **Advanced** button on the Taskbar Properties menu.
14. Click on the **Programs** entry.
15. Left-click on the **Wordpad** icon and drag it to the Startup folder.

FIGURE 29.2 Windows 2000 Start menu properties

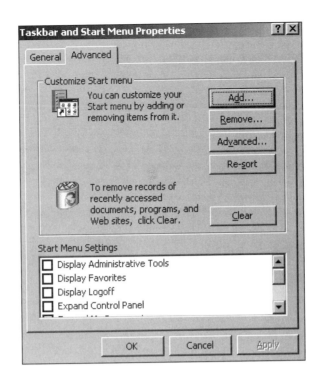

16. Close all open windows on the desktop.
17. Reboot the computer system and note the appearance of the desktop.
18. Open the **Taskbar Properties** window.
19. Select the **Advanced** tab.
20. Select the **Remove** option.
21. Double left-click the **Startup** folder.
22. Select the **Wordpad** icon.
23. Left-click on the **Remove** button.

DISCUSSION AND CONCLUSION

Using a word processor, write your own detailed explanations of the results and observations made during the experiment. To begin, try to say something about each step.

In addition, provide answers to the following questions:

1. What items are located on the Documents folder in the Start menu?
2. Identify the differences between selecting the Open and Explore options.
3. What type of items can be put into the Startup folder?
4. Compare Start menus on each version of Windows and make note of the similarities and differences.

Lab Activity 30
Using the Taskbar

REFERENCE

Exercise 29

INTRODUCTION

In this lab activity, we examine the taskbar, one of the most important elements of the Windows desktop. From the taskbar, the current status of the computer system can be determined at a glance. The taskbar contains the Start button (examined previously), open folders and application programs, and the system tray. Locate each of these items shown in Figure 30.1.

PROCEDURE

TASKBAR PROPERTIES

1. Right-click on a blank section of the taskbar to see the context-sensitive Help menu as shown in Figure 30.2.

FIGURE 30.1 Two views of the taskbar

(a) The taskbar with many applications displayed on one row

(b) The same taskbar resized to two rows

FIGURE 30.2 Context-sensitive time/date menu

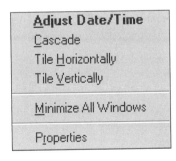

73

FIGURE 30.3   Taskbar Properties window

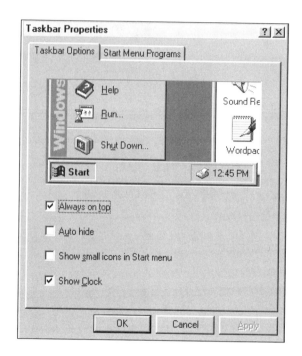

2. Your menu may be different depending on the version of Windows used. Note any differences between the menu shown in Figure 30.2 and the menu on your system.
3. Select the **Properties** menu item to display the Taskbar Properties window as shown in Figure 30.3.
4. Note the settings of the General options on the Taskbar Properties window. Again, note any differences between the window shown in Figure 30.3 and the window displayed on your system.
5. Select the **Auto hide option** and press **OK**.
6. Note the behavior of the taskbar as the pointer is moved on and off the taskbar area of the screen.
7. Right-click and drag the taskbar from the bottom of the screen to the top of the screen. Check the function of the Auto hide feature.
8. Move the taskbar back to the original location on the desktop.
9. Unselect the Auto hide feature.
10. Select each of the options displayed on the menu. Note the behavior of each.
11. Test the operation of each feature, making note of the particular function performed.
12. Deselect each of the options selected in step 10.

THE SYSTEM TRAY

1. Examine the contents of the system tray on your taskbar.
2. Right-click each of the icons and note any menu options that are displayed.
3. Left-click each of the icons and note any menu options that are displayed.

DISCUSSION AND CONCLUSION

Using a word processor, write your own detailed explanations of the results and observations made during the experiment. To begin, try to say something about each step.

In addition, provide answers to the following questions:

1. Is there any indication where the taskbar is located on the desktop when the Auto hide feature is enabled?
2. Compare your version of Windows with different versions. Note any similarities and differences.
3. Are the changes made to the taskbar properties permanent?

Lab Activity 31
Changing the Desktop Properties

REFERENCE

Exercise 29

INTRODUCTION

In this lab activity, we examine the procedures to change the desktop properties. Desktop properties that we will explore include changing the background, screen saver, appearance, and display settings.

PROCEDURE

CHANGING THE DISPLAY BACKGROUND

1. Right-click on an empty section of the display background to display a context-sensitive help menu as shown in Figure 31.1.
2. Note any differences between your context-sensitive help window compared to Figure 31.1.
3. Select the **Properties** option to open the Display Properties window as shown in Figure 31.2.
4. Experiment with the screen background by selecting a different pattern, wallpaper, and Tile/Center option.
5. Select **Apply** to see the changes on the desktop.
6. Repeat steps 4 and 5 to examine the various combinations available.
7. Select **OK** to close the Properties window.

FIGURE 31.1   Desktop help menu

Active Desktop ▸
Arrange Icons ▸
Line Up Icons
Refresh
Paste
Paste Shortcut
New ▸
Properties

FIGURE 31.2 Display
Properties window showing
Background controls

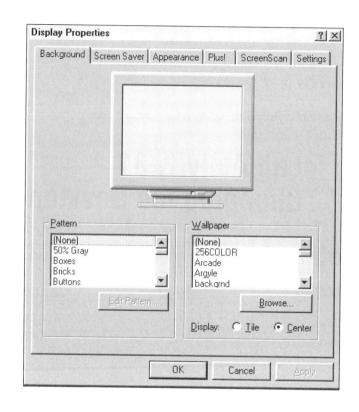

SELECTING A SCREEN SAVER

1. Right-click on an empty section of the display background to display a context-sensitive help menu as shown in Figure 31.1.
2. Select the **Properties** option to open the Display Properties window as shown in Figure 31.2.
3. Select the **Screen Saver** tab to display the screen saver settings.
4. Experiment with the screen saver and energy settings by selecting a different screen saver or energy settings option. *Note:* Review any screen saver settings if they are available.
5. Select **OK** to activate the changes.
6. Confirm the operation of the screen settings.
7. Repeat steps 4 through 6 to examine the various combinations available.
8. Select **OK** to close the Properties window.

CHANGING THE DESKTOP APPEARANCE

1. Right-click on an empty section of the display background to display a context-sensitive help menu as shown in Figure 31.1.
2. Select the **Properties** option to open the Display Properties window.
3. Select the **Appearance** tab to display the appearance settings.
4. Experiment with the schemes, items, and font options by selecting a new scheme, item, or font.
5. Select **Apply** to activate the changes.
6. Repeat steps 4 and 5 to examine the various combinations available.
7. Select **OK** to close the Properties window.

CHANGING THE DISPLAY SETTINGS

1. Right-click on an empty section of the display background to display a context-sensitive help menu as shown in Figure 31.1.

2. Select the **Properties** option to open the Display Properties window as shown in Figure 31.2.
3. Select the **Settings** tab to display the display settings.
4. Note the settings currently active on your monitor.
5. Experiment with the settings by changing the Color Palette and Desktop Area options only.
6. Select **Apply** to activate the changes.
7. Repeat steps 5 and 6 to examine the various combinations available.
8. Select **OK** to close the Properties window.

ADDING A SHORTCUT TO THE DESKTOP

1. Right-click on an empty portion of the desktop.
2. Move the mouse pointer to the New menu selection.
3. Move the mouse pointer to the Shortcut selection on the submenu.
4. Left-click on the **Shortcut** item.
5. Click the **Browse** button.
6. Locate the Windows folder icon (using the scroll bar).
7. Double-click on the **Windows** folder icon.
8. Locate the Calendar icon (using the scroll bar).
9. Left-click on the **Calendar** icon.
10. Left-click the **Open** button.
11. Left-click on the **Next** button.
12. Click on the **Finish** button.
13. Double-click on the **Calendar** icon.
14. Close the Calendar application.

ADDITIONAL PRACTICE ON YOUR OWN

1. Create a shortcut on the desktop to the Calendar application in the Windows directory and demonstrate its use.
2. Experiment with the desktop appearance by choosing five different patterns and five different wallpapers.
3. Compare the centered and tiled options for three different wallpapers.
4. Move the taskbar to all four corners of the display and vary the size. Explain your preference for the normal position of your taskbar.
5. Create several small text files with a text editor or word processor. Put a copy of each file into the Briefcase. Drag the My Briefcase icon onto the icon for your floppy drive. Take your floppy to a different computer and drag the Briefcase from the floppy onto the desktop. Edit the files in the Briefcase. Drag the Briefcase back to the floppy. Put the floppy in the original computer and drag the Briefcase back onto the desktop. Double-click the **My Briefcase** icon and examine its contents. Update the files in any manner you choose.
6. Click the time display on the taskbar. Use the up and down arrows to determine the first and last year recognized by Windows. Can you grab the minute hand and move it around the clock?
7. Enable the Auto hide feature of the taskbar and experiment with the mouse to determine how and when the taskbar will reappear. Resize the taskbar. How large and small can it be?
8. Create a folder on the desktop and name it Temp. Drag some of the other desktop icons into it. Open the Temp folder and drag the icons back to the desktop one at a time. Do the icons snap into place or can you put them anywhere you choose?
9. Open the Recycle Bin. If there are already files in it, determine when they were put there and whether it is safe to delete them. Open a DOS window. Do a directory listing of the current drive and make note of the free space on the drive. Now empty the Recycle Bin. Has the free space changed?

10. Slowly move your mouse pointer over the items in the Programs submenu as if choosing an application to start up. Do you encounter any difficulty trying to select any of the applications?

DISCUSSION AND CONCLUSION

Using a word processor, write your own detailed explanations of the results and observations made during the experiment. To begin, try to say something about each step.

In addition, provide answers to the following questions:

1. How many background combinations are available?
2. How many screen savers are available?
3. How many appearance combinations are available?
4. Do most Windows desktops look the same?
5. Should a screen saver be configured to use a password?

Lab Activity 32
Adjusting the Date and Time

REFERENCE

Exercise 29

INTRODUCTION

In this lab activity, we examine the process used to maintain an accurate time on the computer. The date and time on a computer system is used to record all activity on a computer system. If the date and/or time is inaccurate, it may make it difficult to determine when a certain event occurred or to locate information that was created at a certain time.

One reason why it may be necessary to adjust the date/time is when the system battery is dead and must be replaced. The battery is located on the motherboard and must be replaced with the same type.

In addition to keeping basic time, the time zone and adjustments for daylight savings time are maintained as well. Although the procedure to update the date and time is a simple one, it is also very important.

PROCEDURE

1. Move the mouse pointer over the clock display in the system tray on the taskbar to display the current date as shown in Figure 32.1.
2. Double-click over the time display to show the Date/Time Properties window illustrated in Figure 32.2.
3. Set the computer date to the first date (month and year) available. Note this date.
4. Set the computer date to the last month and year available. Note this date.
5. Set the date and time to the correct values.
6. Select the **Time Zone** tab to review the time zone settings.
7. Left-click on the down arrow on the Time Zone text display shown at the top of the Date/Time Properties window.
8. Left-click and drag the slider to the top of the list. Note the first entry in the list.

FIGURE 32.1   Pop-up date window

FIGURE 32.2 Date/Time
Properties window

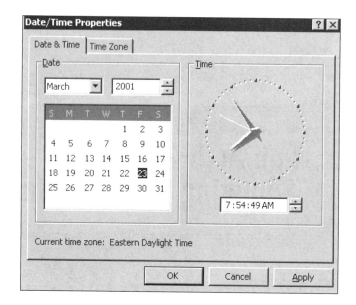

9. Left-click and drag the slider to the bottom of the list. Note the last entry in the list.
10. Set the computer date/time to a few minutes before midnight on a day when daylight savings time is about to start or end.
11. Reboot the computer system after the date has changed. Note any messages displayed during startup.
12. Reset the date and time to their proper values.

DISCUSSION AND CONCLUSION

Using a word processor, write your own detailed explanations of the results and observations made during the experiment. To begin, try to say something about each step.

In addition, provide answers to the following questions:

1. Why is it important to keep the date and time correct on a computer system?
2. Explain how the system date application can be used as a calendar.
3. Why is it important to set the correct time zone?

Lab Activity 33
Using Windows Explorer

REFERENCE

Exercise 31

INTRODUCTION

In this lab activity, we examine Windows Explorer, the program used to display the contents of any disks connected to a computer system.

PROCEDURE

1. Locate Windows Explorer in the Start menu. Since the location will be different depending on what version of Windows you are using, note the location.
2. Start the **Windows Explorer** program.
3. Compare the Windows Explorer display against Figure 33.1. Note any differences.
4. Select the **Toolbars** option from the View pull-down menu. Note the toolbars with a check mark next to them.
5. Enable/disable the toolbars one at a time and note the effect on the Explorer display window.
6. Compare the items on the pull-down menus with the options available on the toolbar. List the options that appear in both. List the options that appear only in a pull-down menu.
7. Locate the pull-down menu that contains **Folder Options**.
8. Examine the contents of the Folder Options window. List the names of each tab.
9. Select the **View** tab.
10. Note the setting for each of the options available.
11. Enable/disable the settings for each of the options. Note the effect in Windows Explorer.
12. Select the **File Types** tab.
13. Note the items in the text box.
14. Close the Folder Options window.
15. Close the Windows Explorer application.

FIGURE 33.1 (a) Windows 98
Explorer window and
(b) Windows 2000 Explorer
window

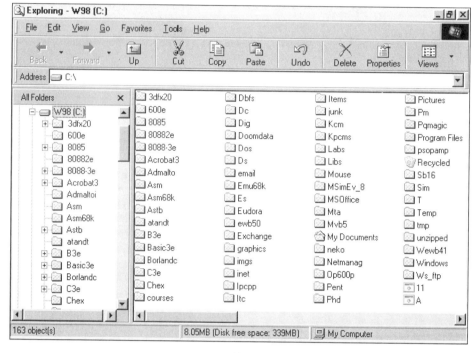

(a)

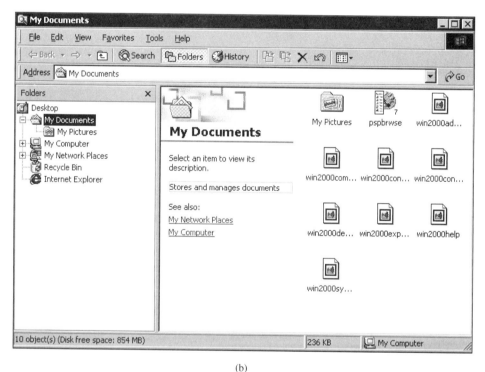

(b)

**DISCUSSION AND
CONCLUSION**

Using a word processor, write your own detailed explanations of the results and observations made during the experiment. To begin, try to say something about each step.

In addition, provide answers to the following questions:

1. How are hidden files protected by Windows Explorer?
2. Where does My Documents appear in the Windows Explorer display? Does it appear more than once?
3. How is Windows Explorer used in the Start menu?

Lab Activity 34
Working with Files and Folders

REFERENCE

Exercises 31 and 33

INTRODUCTION

In this lab activity, we examine the process of working with files and folders. As the Windows operating system is installed, the files which comprise the operating system are located inside folders that make it very easy to keep track of the related items. It is recommended that computer users also keep track of their files in the same way by grouping related files together. Almost every application program is designed to work with files such as creating new files, working with old files, and organizing them into folders.

PROCEDURE

CREATING A NEW FILE

1. Left-click on the **Start** menu and select the **Programs** folder.
2. Select the **Accessories** folder on the Programs folder to open the **Notepad** application (shown in Figure 34.1).
3. Enter **'A+ Certification is very important'**.
4. Click the **File** pull-down menu and select the **Save** option.
5. Note the folder name where the file will be saved.
6. Enter **aplusfile.txt** in the file name field.
7. Click the **Save** button.
8. Exit from the Notepad application.

FIGURE 34.1   Notepad window

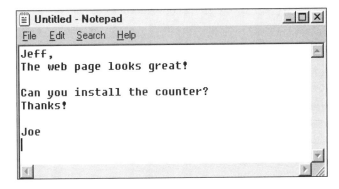

RENAMING A FILE (METHOD 1)

1. Open **Windows Explorer**.
2. Navigate to the location where the aplusfile.txt text file was created.
3. Right-click on the file name and select **Rename**.
4. Enter **aplus.txt** and press the **Enter** key.

RENAMING A FILE (METHOD 2)

1. Open the **Notepad** application program.
2. Select **Open...** from the file pull-down menu.
3. Right-click on the **aplus.txt** text file.
4. Select the **Rename** option.
5. Enter **a+** and press **Enter**.
6. Note any messages displayed.
7. Select the **No** option.
8. Enter **a+.txt** and press **Enter**.

COPYING A FILE

1. Open **Windows Explorer**.
2. Navigate to the folder where a+.txt is stored.
3. Right-click on the file **a+.txt**.
4. Click the **Copy** option.
5. Right-click on the blank area next to the a+.txt file.
6. Select the **Paste** option from the menu.
7. Note the name of the copied file.

CREATING A FOLDER

1. Open the **Windows Explorer** application.
2. Select **New** from the File pull-down menu.
3. Select **Folder**.
4. Enter **a plus files** for the folder name.
5. Note the location of the folder.

COPY FILES TO THE NEW FOLDER

1. Press and hold the **Control** key on the keyboard.
2. Left-click the file **a+.txt**.
3. Left-click the **Copy of a+.txt** text file.
4. Release the Control key.
5. Drag the files to the new folder.
6. Verify the contents of the folder.

DELETING FILES AND FOLDERS

1. Right-click on the **a plus files** folder.
2. Select **Delete** from the File pull-down menu.
3. Confirm that you wish to delete the folder by selecting the **Yes** option.
4. Examine the contents of the Recycle Bin.
5. Empty the Recycle Bin.

DISCUSSION AND CONCLUSION

Using a word processor, write your own detailed explanations of the results and observations made during the experiment. To begin, try to say something about each step.

In addition, provide answers to the following questions:

1. Is it easier to use Windows Explorer or Notepad to rename a file?
2. Does it make a difference where the pointer is located when performing a file copy?
3. What is the purpose of using the control key when dragging files to the new folder?

Lab Activity 35
Using Accessories

REFERENCE

Exercise 33

INTRODUCTION

In this lab activity, we examine the Windows Accessories folder. There are many programs that can be used for both new and experienced users. Figure 35.1 shows three screen shots of the Accessories menus on different versions of Windows.

Notice the similarities and differences between the Accessories folders. You are encouraged to review and experiment with all of the programs to determine their usefulness.

FIGURE 35.1 (a) Typical Windows 95/98 Accessories menu

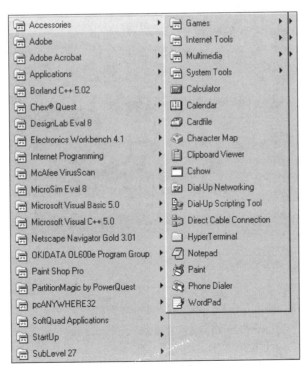

(a)

(continued on the next page)

FIGURE 35.1 *(continued)*
(b) Windows NT Accessories menu, and (c) Windows 2000 Accessories menu

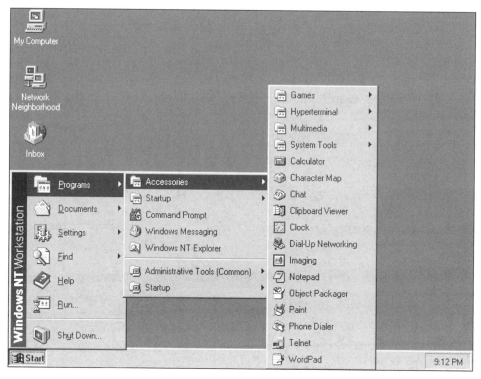

(b)

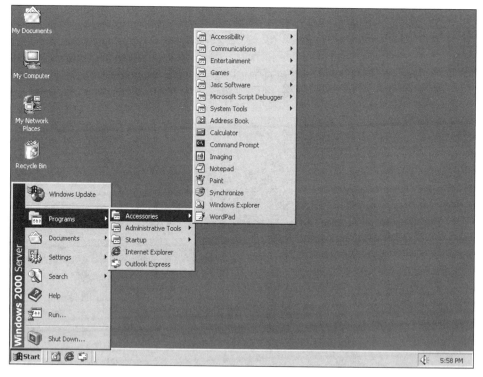

(c)

PROCEDURE

1. Open the **Accessories** folder on the Start menu.
2. Note any differences between your accessories and the Accessories menu shown in Figure 35.1.
3. Review the contents for each of the folders shown in the Accessories menu. List each folder name and the contents.
4. Run each of the programs in the Communications folder and review the contents of the on-line help for each application.

5. Run each of the programs in the Entertainment folder and review the contents of the on-line help for each application.
6. Perform each of the following steps using the programs found in the Entertainment folder:
   a. Play a CD using the CD Player.
   b. Open several of the media files using the Media Player.
   c. Record some audio using the Sound Recorder if a microphone is available.
7. Run each of the programs in the System Tools folder and review the contents of the on-line help for each application.
8. Perform each of the following steps using programs found in the System Tools folder:
   a. Perform a disk cleanup.
   b. Defragment the system disk.
   c. Run a thorough test of the system disk using the Scandisk application.
   d. Review the contents of the System Information to identify the processor type and available system memory.
9. Open the calculator.
10. Select the scientific display from the View pull-down menu.
11. Select **Hex numbers**.
12. Enter **FFFF**.
13. Select the **Decimal numbers** button to convert the hex number into decimal. Record the result.
14. Close the calculator.
15. Compare the Imaging tool with the Paint program.
16. Compare the Notepad tool with Wordpad.

ADDITIONAL PRACTICE ON YOUR OWN

1. Use Netscape or Internet Explorer to browse the Web. Try www.windows95.com or www.winfiles.com, two very good sites for Windows users.
2. Check the amount of fragmentation for each drive on your lab system. If you have a floppy disk, check it also.
3. If approved by your instructor, defragment each drive. Make note of how long it takes to do a single drive and the size of the drive.
4. Determine the amount of available resources (system, user, GDI).
5. Use the System Monitor to watch at least four parameters (processor usage, etc.) for 10 minutes. Perform other work on the system as you watch the display. What do you notice?
6. Use the Calculator to determine how long, in minutes, a photon of light takes to travel from the sun to the earth. The distance is 93 million miles and the speed of light is 186,000 miles/second.
7. Make a cardfile of your favorite television shows. Explain how you organized them.
8. Open the **Clipboard Viewer**. Is there anything on it? If so, where do you think the data came from?
9. Use Notepad to write a short letter requesting a sample catalog from a computer manufacturer. Print out the final version.
10. Open the letter from step 9 using WordPad. Use the text editing features to make some words bold, others italic, and others a different size. Center and right justify some of the text. Print out the final version.
11. Explore each of the Windows NT Administrative Tools on the Administrative Tools display menu.

DISCUSSION AND CONCLUSION

Using a word processor, write your own detailed explanations of the results and observations made during the experiment. To begin, try to say something about each step.

In addition, provide answers to the following questions:

1. Which are the most important accessories for a new user?

2. Which of the accessories can be used to help manage the computer?
3. What is the advantage of knowing about and using the accessories?
4. What programs does the Maintenance Wizard maintain?
5. Explain why a user should be familiar with all of the system tools.

Lab Activity 36
Using the Control Panel

REFERENCE

Exercise 30

INTRODUCTION

In this lab activity, we examine the Control Panel. Using the Control Panel (shown in Figure 36.1), virtually every aspect of the Windows operating system can be examined and modified. Being familiar with each Control Panel program is crucial to a good understanding of Windows. Because several of the Control Panel settings are covered in other lab exercises, this experiment will focus on items not covered elsewhere.

PROCEDURE

1. Open the **Control Panel** using the **Settings** option on the Start menu.
2. Compare the icons shown in your Control Panel to the Control Panel shown in Figure 36.1. Note any differences.

FIGURE 36.1 (a) Windows 95 Control Panel

(a)

(continued on the next page)

FIGURE 36.1 *(continued)*
(b) Windows 98 Control Panel,
(c) Windows NT 4.0 Control
Panel (Web-style format), and
(d) Windows 2000 Control Panel

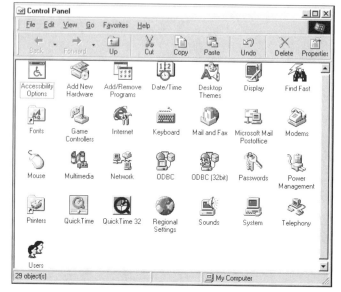

(b)

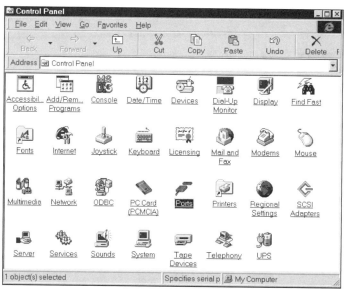

(c)

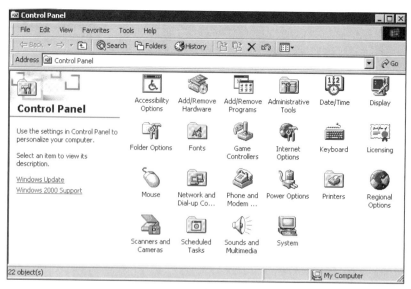

(d)

3. Review the Accessibility properties.
  a. Note the current Accessibility properties settings.
  b. One at a time, enable/display Accessibility settings and note the result.
4. Review the system Fonts.
  a. Note the number of fonts available.
  b. Double-click on several of the fonts.
  c. Note the names, file sizes, and versions of each font examined.
5. Review the Keyboard properties.
  a. Note the current Keyboard settings.
  b. Modify each of the settings, one at a time, and note the result.
  c. Return the Keyboard settings to the original settings.
6. Review the Mouse properties.
  a. Note the current Mouse settings.
  b. Modify each of the settings, one at a time, and note the result.
  c. Return the Mouse settings to the original settings.
7. Review the Password properties settings.
  a. Note the current Password properties.
  b. Change the current password.
  c. Enable remote administration of the computer system.
  d. Modify the User Profile settings.
  e. Restore the original Password properties.
8. Review the Power Management settings.
  a. Note the current Power Management settings.
  b. Modify each of the settings, one at a time, and note the result.
  c. Return the Power Management settings to the original settings.
9. Review the Regional settings.
  a. Note the current Regional settings.
  b. Modify each of the settings, one at a time, and note the result.
  c. Return the Regional settings to the original settings.
10. Review the Sound properties.
  a. Play several of the sounds available.
  b. Note the Programs listed.
  c. Add a new sound to an event not linked to a sound.
  d. Verify the operation.
  e. Remove the sound associated in step c.
11. Review the Telephony properties.
  a. Note the current Telephony settings.
  b. Add a new dialing location.
  c. Add a new Calling Card.
  d. Note the currently installed Telephony drivers.
12. Review the Users settings.
  a. Add a new user for the computer system called APLUS.
  b. Do not create a password for the user.
  c. Log off the current system user.
  d. Log on using the user name APLUS.
  e. Add a password for the user APLUS.
  f. Log off the computer system.
  g. Log on using the user name APLUS.
  h. Select **OK** without entering the password. Note the result.
  i. Log on using the correct password.

DISCUSSION AND CONCLUSION

Using a word processor, write your own detailed explanations of the results and observations made during the experiment. To begin, try to say something about each step.

In addition, provide answers to the following questions:

1. List the most important Control Panel utilities.

2. Explain why it is important to know the current system settings.
3. Which of the Control Panel utilities should be restricted?
4. Which of the Control Panel utilities should be accessible?
5. Which of the Control Panel utilities should users be encouraged to modify?

Lab Activity 37
Examining the Multimedia Settings

REFERENCE

Exercise 30

INTRODUCTION

In this lab activity, we examine the Multimedia properties. Windows provides drivers for many multimedia devices. The properties of these devices are controlled using the Multimedia or Sounds and Multimedia Control Panel applications.

PROCEDURE

MULTIMEDIA SOFTWARE PROPERTIES

1. Open the **Control Panel**.
2. Double-click on the **Multimedia** (or **Sounds and Multimedia**) icon to open the Multimedia properties shown in Figure 37.1.
3. Compare the Multimedia properties on your system to the one shown in Figure 37.1. Note any differences.
4. Identify the preferred device for playback.
5. Identify the preferred device for recording.
6. Check the pull-down options for the preferred recording and playback devices. Are any other options available? List them.
7. Review the contents of the other tabs shown on the Multimedia Properties display window.
8. Select the **Advanced** (or **Devices**) tab.
9. Examine the properties for each of the devices listed.
10. Close the Multimedia Properties window.

MULTIMEDIA HARDWARE PROPERTIES

1. Open the **Control Panel**.
2. Double-click on the **System** icon to open the System Properties window.
3. Select the **Device Manager** tab to display a list of system devices similar to what is shown in Figure 37.2.
4. Note any differences between the System properties shown in Figure 37.2 and the System properties on your system.

FIGURE 37.1   Multimedia Properties menu

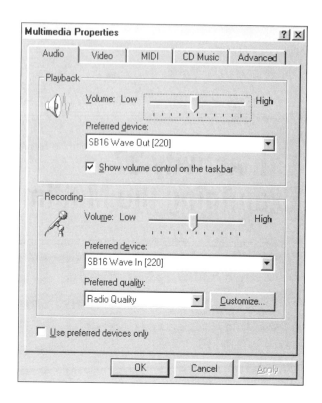

FIGURE 37.2   System Properties reports an error

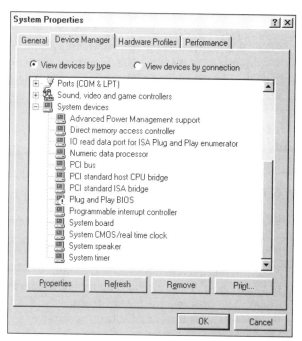

5. Locate the **Sound, Video, and Game Controllers** option from the list.
6. Examine the Sound Card settings. Note the type of sound card installed.
7. Determine the hardware settings for your sound card. Identify the following items:
   - IRQ
   - I/O port address
   - Driver file
   - DMA controller
8. Compare the items listed in step 7 with the software properties listed previously.
9. Examine the properties for each of the items listed in the Sound, Video, and Game Controllers.
10. Close the System Properties window.

Using a word processor, write your own detailed explanations of the results and observations made during the experiment. To begin, try to say something about each step.

In addition, provide answers to the following questions:

1. Did you notice a way to add volume control to the system tray on the taskbar?
2. What is the purpose of a CODEC?
3. What type of volume control is provided to the computer user?
4. What are the advantages of using a sound card in a computer?

Lab Activity 38
Using a Network Printer

REFERENCE

Exercise 32

INTRODUCTION

In this lab activity, we examine a network printer. A network printer may or may not be connected to a computer, since some printers contain a built-in network card allowing them to be attached directly to the network.

This activity is based on a Hewlett Packard printer. Your instructor may substitute a different printer that is available in the lab.

PROCEDURE

INSTALLING A LOCAL PRINTER FOR USE ON THE NETWORK

1. From the Start Menu, select the **Settings** option.
2. Select **Printers** to display the Printers folder, as shown in Figure 38.1.
3. Compare your Printers folder to the one shown in Figure 38.1. Note any differences.
4. Select the **Add Printer** icon to start the printer wizard.
5. Select the **Next** button.
6. Select the **Local Printer** radio button.
7. Select **HP** as the printer manufacturer.
8. Select any HP printer from the list.
9. Press the **Next** button.
10. Select the **LPT1** port and press the **Next** button.

FIGURE 38.1   **Printers folder**

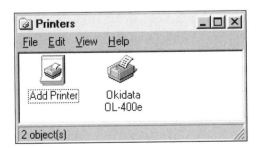

FIGURE 38.2   Giving network
access to your printer

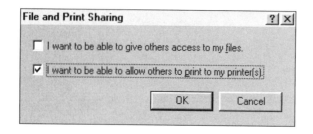

11. Enter a name for the HP printer (or use the default).
12. Select **Yes** to make this printer the default printer.
13. Press the **Finish** button.
14. Supply the Windows CD-ROM for the required drivers if prompted.
15. Note the result of adding a printer by examining the Printers folder.

For Windows 95/98 computer systems
16. Right-click the **Network Neighborhood** icon on the desktop.
17. Select the **Properties** option to display the Network Properties menu.
18. Select the **File and Print Sharing** button to display the window shown in Figure 38.2.
19. Left-click on the box next to the text line, "I want to be able to allow others to print to my printer(s)."
20. Click the **OK** button.
21. Click the **OK** button to close the Network Properties window.
22. Reboot the computer (if necessary) to allow access to the system printer(s).

INSTALLING A NETWORK PRINTER

1. From the Start Menu, select the **Settings** option.
2. Select **Printers** to display the Printers folder as shown in Figure 38.1.
3. Compare your Printers folder to the one shown in Figure 38.1. Note any differences.
4. Select the **Add Printer** icon to start the printer wizard.
5. Select the **Next** button.
6. Select the **Network Printer** radio button.
7. Enter **\\aplus\hp6l** in the Network Path (or queue name) text box.
8. Select **No** to allow printing from DOS programs.
9. Select the **Next** option. Note any messages that are displayed.
10. Select **HP** as the printer manufacturer.
11. Select any HP printer from the list.
12. Press the **Next** button.
13. Enter a name for the HP printer (or use the default).
14. Select **Yes** to make this printer the default printer.
15. Press the **Finish** button.
16. Supply the Windows CD-ROM for the required drivers if prompted.
17. Note the result of adding a printer by examining the Printers folder.

CHECKING PRINTER PROPERTIES

1. From the Start Menu, select **Settings**.
2. Select **Printers** from the Settings menu.
3. Right-click on the **Printer** icon if you wish to check the properties.
4. Select **Properties** from the menu.
5. Review each of the Printer properties and available settings.
6. Close the Printer Properties window.

PRINTING ON A NETWORK PRINTER

1. Open the **Notepad** application program on the Accessories menu.
2. Enter some text into the Notepad.
3. Select **Page Setup** from the File pull-down menu.
4. Select the **Printer** button.
5. Verify that the proper printer has been selected.
6. Select **Print** from the File pull-down menu.

DELETING A PRINTER

1. Open the **Printers** folder.
2. Right-click on the printer to be deleted.
3. Select **Delete** from the list of menu options.
4. Select the **Yes** button to confirm the Delete operation.
5. Select **Yes** to delete files used only by this printer (if prompted).

DISCUSSION AND CONCLUSION

Using a word processor, write your own detailed explanations of the results and observations made during the experiment. To begin, try to say something about each step.

In addition, provide answers to the following questions:

1. How many printers can be installed on a computer system?
2. What is the difference between a network printer and a local printer?
3. If a printer is deleted accidentally, what must be done to restore it?
4. Install several other printers on your own and note the features.

Lab Activity 39
Using the Network Neighborhood

REFERENCE

Exercise 34

INTRODUCTION

In this lab activity, we examine the Network Neighborhood. Using the Network Neighborhood, it is possible to determine what resources are available on the network. If the Network Neighborhood is available, it is a good indication that the network is functioning properly; otherwise, it is an indication of an error.

PROCEDURE

WINDOWS 95/98/NT

1. Select **Log off** from the Start menu or the Shutdown menu.
2. Select **Cancel** on the logon screen, bypassing the logon procedure.
3. Note any error messages that are displayed and press **OK** to continue.
4. If the logon prompt reappears, make a note of it and continue on to step 8.
5. Double-click on the **Network Neighborhood** icon on the desktop.
6. Note any messages that are displayed.
7. Select **Log off** from the Start menu or the Shutdown menu.
8. Enter a valid user name and password at the system logon prompts and press the **OK** button.
9. Double-click on the **Network Neighborhood** icon on the desktop to display a window similar to the one shown in Figure 39.1.
10. Note the contents of the Network Neighborhood window.
11. Double-click on each of the resources listed in the Network Neighborhood display. Note the name of the computer system and the type of resource it is displaying, plus the name of the displayed resource.
12. Right-click on each of the resources listed in the Network Neighborhood to examine the properties. Note the results.
13. Connect to a networked printer and print a document.
14. Connect to and examine the contents of a network drive using Windows Explorer.
15. Disconnect from any network printers or shared disk drives.

FIGURE 39.1 Network Neighborhood window

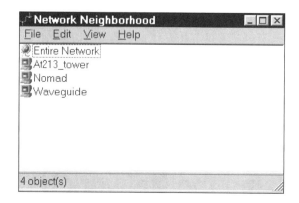

WINDOWS 2000

1. Double-click on the **Network Places** icon.
2. List the contents of the Network Places display.
3. Double-click on the **Entire Network** icon.
4. List the contents of the Entire Network display.
5. Double-click on each of the network resources listed and note the results.
6. Right-click on each of the network resources listed and note the results.

DISCUSSION AND CONCLUSION

Using a word processor, write your own detailed explanations of the results and observations made during the experiment. To begin, try to say something about each step.

In addition, provide answers to the following questions:

1. Is it possible to view the contents of the Network Neighborhood without logging on to Windows?
2. What types of resources are listed in the Network Neighborhood display?
3. Are all of the Network Resources listed in the Network Neighborhood?

Lab Activity 40
Sharing Files and Folders

REFERENCE

Exercises 31 and 34

INTRODUCTION

In this lab activity, we examine the process of sharing files and folders. On a Windows 95/98 computer with FAT 16/32, only drives and folders can be shared. On a Windows NT computer with NTFS, formatted disks, drives, folders, and individual files may be shared.

PROCEDURE

WINDOWS 95/98

1. Open **Windows Explorer** or double-click the **My Computer** icon on the desktop.
2. Right-click on the **C:** drive.
3. If the menu contains a sharing option, proceed to step 12.
4. Right-click the **Network Neighborhood** icon on the desktop.
5. Select the **Properties** option to display the Network Properties menu.
6. Select the **File and Print Sharing** button to display the window shown in Figure 40.1.
7. Left-click on the box next to the text line, "I want to be able to give others access to my file(s)."
8. Click the **OK** button.
9. Click the **OK** button to close the Network Properties window.
10. Reboot the computer (if necessary) to allow access to the system printer(s).
11. Open **Windows Explorer**.

FIGURE 40.1 Giving network access to your files and printer

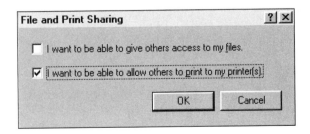

**FIGURE 40.2 Sharing
Properties window for drive D:**

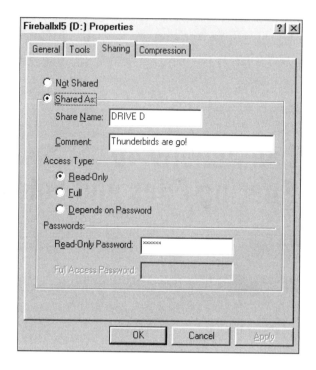

12. Right-click on the **C:** drive.
13. Select **Properties** from the context-sensitive menu to display the Disk Properties window as shown in Figure 40.2.
14. Examine the contents of the Disk Properties sharing settings and note any differences.
15. Select the **Shared As** radio button.
16. Enter **C: Disk** in the Share Name field.
17. Enter **Shared C disk** in the Comment field.
18. Verify that **Read-Only** Access Type is selected.
19. Enter **aplus** in the Read-Only Password field.
20. Press the **OK** button.
21. Re-enter the **Read-Only Password** setting when prompted.
22. Note the change in the C: drive icon in the Explorer display.

WINDOWS NT/2000

1. Open **Windows Explorer** or double-click on the **My Computer** icon on the desktop.
2. Right-click on the **C:** drive.
3. Select **Properties** from the context-sensitive menu to display the Disk Properties window as shown in Figure 40.3.
4. Examine the contents of the Disk Properties sharing settings and note any differences.
5. Select the **New Share** radio button.
6. Enter **C Disk** in the Share Name field.
7. Enter **Shared C disk** in the Comment field.
8. Select the **Permissions** button.
9. Remove the check boxes for Full Control and Change to make the disk read-only.
10. Press the **OK** button.
11. Select the **Share Name** down arrow. Make a note of the shares available.
12. Note the change in the C: drive icon in the Explorer display.

MAPPING A SHARED DRIVE

1. Open **Windows Explorer**.
2. Select **Map Network Drive** from the Tools pull-down menu.

**FIGURE 40.3 Windows 2000
Disk Sharing Properties**

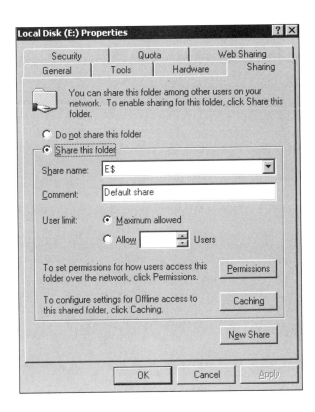

3. Select the **Browse** option.
4. Select a shared disk from the list of available resources.
5. Supply a password if required.
6. Close Windows Explorer.
7. Open **My Computer**.
8. Examine the icon for shared network disks.
9. Copy and paste files between the local disk and the network disk.

**DISCUSSION AND
CONCLUSION**

Using a word processor, write your own detailed explanations of the results and observations made during the experiment. To begin, try to say something about each step.

In addition, provide answers to the following questions:

1. What types of security problems do shared disks pose?
2. Are network disks treated the same as a local disk in Windows?
3. Is it a good idea to restrict access to a shared disk?
4. What are the advantages of allowing write access to a shared disk?

Lab Activity 41
Using PING, TRACERT,
and WINIPCFG

REFERENCE

Exercise 45

INTRODUCTION

In this lab activity, we examine three useful network application programs.

PROCEDURE

PING

1. Search for help on the PING program. Note the number of topics returned.
2. Open a DOS window.
3. Enter **PING** and press **Enter**. Note the results.
4. PING all of the following addresses:
   - www.yahoo.com
   - www.intel.com
   - www.whitehouse.gov
   - www.nasa.gov
   - 192.203.131.137
   (using the format **ping www.yahoo.com**)
   Make a note of the address and the response time for each.
5. PING an additional five addresses of your choice. List each of the addresses you choose.
6. If possible, PING the same addresses at a different time of the day. State your findings.

TRACERT

1. Search for help on the TRACERT program. Note the number of topics returned.
2. Open a DOS window.
3. Enter **TRACERT** and press **Enter**. Note the results.
4. Run TRACERT on these addresses:
   - www.yahoo.com
   - www.intel.com

- www.whitehouse.gov
- www.nasa.gov
- 192.203.131.137

Create a table of the number of hops to each address. Make a note of any other information that you find interesting.

5. TRACERT to another 5 addresses of your own choice. List each of the addresses that you choose. Add these addresses to the table created for step 4.

WINIPCFG ON WINDOWS 95/98

1. Open a DOS window.
2. Enter **winipcfg** and press **Enter**.
3. Note the current IP address and hardware address.
4. Select the **Advanced** button.
5. Determine the lease of the DHCP address for your computer.

IPCONFIG ON WINDOWS NT/2000

1. Open a DOS window.
2. Enter **ipconfig** and press **Enter**.
3. Note the current IP address and hardware address.
4. Enter **ipconfig –h** to obtain help on the ipconfig utility.
5. Enter **ipconfig /all** to examine all IP configuration information.
6. Determine the lease of the DHCP address for your computer.

DISCUSSION AND CONCLUSION

Using a word processor, write your own detailed explanations of the results and observations made during the experiment. To begin, try to say something about each step.

In addition, provide answers to the following questions:

1. What is the purpose of the PING application program?
2. What is the purpose of the TRACERT application program?
3. What are the purposes of the WINIPCFG and IPCONFIG application programs?

Lab Activity 42
Getting Started with E-mail

REFERENCE

Exercise 47

INTRODUCTION

In this lab activity, we examine electronic mail, one of the most popular network application programs. Examine the e-mail program shown in Figure 42.1. Using e-mail, users around the world can communicate almost instantaneously 24 hours a day.

Although this lab exercise uses Outlook Express as the e-mail client program, other e-mail clients may be substituted. Each client will require the same information to operate properly.

FIGURE 42.1 Microsoft Outlook Express displaying a message

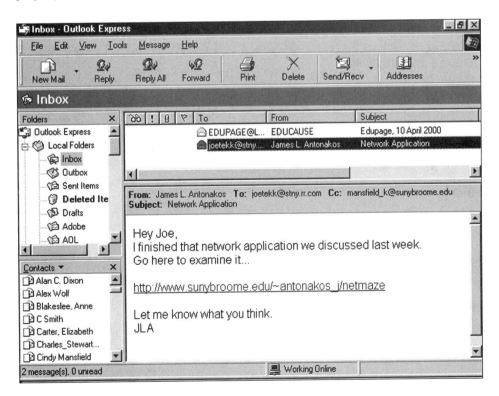

DETERMINING BASIC E-MAIL INFORMATION

1. Obtain your e-mail address from your instructor or system administrator.
2. Search the system for help on Electronic Mail and Outlook Express.

CONFIGURING AN E-MAIL CLIENT

1. Open the **Outlook Express** e-mail program.
2. Select **Accounts** from the Tools pull-down menu.
3. Select the **Add** option.
4. Enter your **name**.
5. Select the **Next** button.
6. Enter your **e-mail address**.
7. Verify that the incoming mail setting is set to POP.
8. Enter the **incoming** and **outgoing mail server address**.
9. Select the **Next** button.
10. Specify the **account name** and **password**.
11. Select the **Next** button.
12. Select the **Finish** button.
13. Right-click on the account you just created that is now displayed in the list.
14. Select the **Properties** option to display a window similar to the one shown in Figure 42.2.
15. Review the information on each of the tabs on the Properties display.
16. Close the Properties window.

SENDING E-MAIL MESSAGES

1. Create and send an e-mail message to an invalid mailbox. What type of error message is generated?
2. Create and send an e-mail message to an invalid computer. What type of error message is generated?

FIGURE 42.2 Outlook Express general e-mail properties

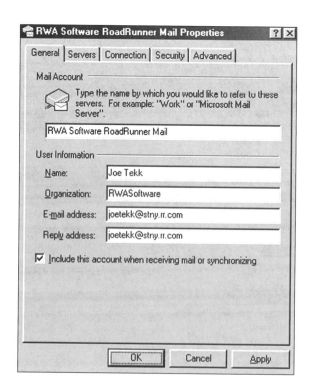

3. Create and send a message with a text attachment.
4. Create and send a message with a binary attachment.
5. Examine the contents of the Outbox and Sent Items folders.

RECEIVING E-MAIL MESSAGES

1. Arrange for a lab partner to send several e-mail messages to you (with and without attachments).
2. Examine the contents of the Inbox.
3. Left-click on the e-mail message to review.
4. Note if the message contains an attachment.
5. Open the e-mail attachment by left-clicking on it. *Note:* Only open an e-mail attachment when you are confident it does not contain a virus.
6. Save the e-mail attachment to disk.

CREATING FOLDERS TO STORE MESSAGES

1. Right-click on the **Local Folders** item in the list of folders.
2. Select **New Folder**.
3. Enter **Aplus** (or other appropriate text) as the name for the folder.
4. Position the mouse over the e-mail message.
5. Left-click and hold the mouse while dragging the message into the folder.
6. Note the result of performing these steps.

DISCUSSION AND CONCLUSION

Using a word processor, write your own detailed explanations of the results and observations made during the experiment. To begin, try to say something about each step.

In addition, provide answers to the following questions:

1. What type of system help is available for e-mail?
2. Do the messages returned due to an error condition adequately identify the different types of errors?
3. What happens if your e-mail address changes? Which fields would need to be updated in Outlook Express?

Lab Activity 43
Using FTP and Telnet

REFERENCE

Exercise 44

INTRODUCTION

In this lab activity, we examine two common TCP/IP protocols: FTP and Telnet. Using these network application programs, it is possible to make a connection to a remote computer using Telnet and transfer files between computers using FTP.

The FTP process is handy when downloading device driver updates from the Web. Telnet can be useful when it is necessary to connect to a resource to receive more information.

PROCEDURE

1. Contact your local computer center and ask if there is FTP and Telnet service available. Record the corresponding network addresses for each service.
2. Use the Windows FTP client (or another FTP client of your choice) to connect to an FTP site.
3. Transfer a text file using the ASCII transfer mode.
4. Examine the size of the original text file and the size of the transferred file. Are they the same?
5. Repeat steps 3 and 4, except transfer the text file using the binary mode.
6. Transfer a binary file using both the ASCII and binary transfer modes. Examine the size of the original and the sizes of both transferred files. Note any differences.
7. Quit the FTP client.
8. Run the FTP client again and enter a STAT command before, during, and after an FTP session is established. What information is different? What information stays the same?
9. Use Telnet to connect to your computer center's mainframe. Log all session activity to a file.
10. Use Telnet to connect to the Library of Congress at **locis.loc.gov**. Log all session activity to a file.

DISCUSSION AND CONCLUSION

Using a word processor, write your own detailed explanations of the results and observations made during the experiment. To begin, try to say something about each step.

In addition, provide answers to the following questions:

1. Why use FTP to transfer files rather than e-mail?
2. What happens if a text file is transferred as binary or a binary file is transfered as text using FTP?
3. What advantages does a Telnet session have over using an ordinary ASCII data terminal?
4. What type of information about FTP and Telnet is available on the Web?

Lab Activity 44
Scanning for Viruses

REFERENCE

Exercise 38

INTRODUCTION

In this lab activity, we examine computer viruses, one of the most common threats to a personal computer system.

    Because a virus scanner is not included with the Windows operating system, it is necessary to purchase a product from a third party such as McAfee, Norton, etc. Most of these products offer a free trial version of their software from the Web. For the purposes of this lab activity, the McAfee VirusScan product will be used.

PROCEDURE

DOWNLOADING A VIRUS SCANNER

1. Open a browser such as **Internet Explorer**.
2. Enter **www.mcafee.com** in the address field.
3. Select the **Downloads** option.
4. Select the **Free service/evaluation software** option.
5. Select the **VirusScan download**.
6. Enter your **e-mail address**, **name**, and **postal code** as required.
7. Select the **Save** option to save the file to disk. Note the directory where the downloaded file will be stored.
8. Wait for the download to complete.
9. Select **Run** from the Start menu.
10. Browse to the directory where the downloaded executable file was stored.
11. Double-click on the downloaded file.
12. Select **OK** on the Run window to run the downloaded file.
13. Select the default options from the Windows InstallShield program to begin the installation process.
14. Reboot the computer when prompted.
15. Select the default options from the VirusScan setup program by selecting the **Next** option.
16. Perform a Typical Installation by selecting the **Next** button.

17. Select the **Finish** button to begin the installation.
18. Note the activities that take place during the installation process.
19. If blank floppy disks are available, create a set of rescue disks.
20. Note the contents of the desktop and the system tray after the installation.

SCANNING FOR VIRUSES

1. Double-click on the **McAfee VirusScan** desktop icon.
2. Click the **Scan** option.
3. Note the Where and What menu settings.
4. Click on the **Settings** button to review the program settings.
5. Click **OK** to return to the VirusScan program.
6. Click the **Scan Now** button. Note any messages that are displayed.
7. Click **OK** when the scan is complete. Note the number of files scanned and the number of files infected.
8. Exit from the VirusScan program.

UPDATING THE VIRUS SCANNER DATA FILES

1. Double-click on the **McAfee VirusScan** desktop icon.
2. Select the **Update** button.
3. Select **Next** to begin the update process.
4. Fill in the Registration Form and select the **Next** button.
5. Make a note of the number of updates applied.
6. Enter **Y** to reboot the computer when prompted.
7. Perform the steps in Scanning for Viruses after the computer system has restarted.

DISCUSSION AND CONCLUSION

Using a word processor, write your own detailed explanations of the results and observations made during the experiment. To begin, try to say something about each step.

In addition, provide answers to the following questions:

1. How often must the virus scanner be updated?
2. How does the computer user know that the virus scanner is active?
3. What happens if the scanner detects a virus?
4. Why is it important for a computer to have a virus scanner installed?

Lab Activity 45
Installing and Upgrading Windows

REFERENCE

Exercises 27, 28, and 35

INTRODUCTION

In this lab activity, we examine the process of installing and upgrading the Windows operating system. When upgrading an operating system, all new operating system files are placed in the same directory as the current operating system. When installing a new operating system, all operating system files are placed in a new directory. In a dual boot system, two or more directories containing separate operating systems exist.

PROCEDURE

INSTALLATION CHECKLIST

1. Check system requirements by reading the Read1st.txt, Readme.doc, and any hardware compatibility information. Refer to Table 45.1 for several Windows minimum requirements.
2. Insert the first installation floppy disk in the A: drive.
3. Turn on the computer system's power.
4. Insert the Windows installation CD-ROM.
5. Insert other installation floppy disks in the A: drive as directed by the installation process.
6. Accept the License Agreement.

TABLE 45.1 Minimum installation requirements

Operating System	Processor	Minimum RAM	Maximum Hard Disk Space
95	386DX	4MB	55MB
98	486DX-66	16MB	295MB
ME	Pentium-150	32MB	645MB
NT Server	486DX-25	16MB	124MB
2000 Server	Pentium-133	32MB	650MB

TABLE 45.2   Upgrade paths for Windows operating systems

From	To 95	To 98	To ME	To NT	To 2000
3.x	✔	✔			
95		✔	✔		✔
98			✔		✔
NT					✔

7. Select a location on the hard drive for the operating system. On a new hard drive, a new partition must be created. If the new operating system is installed on a disk containing an existing operating system, a dual boot system is created.
8. Format the partition if required.
9. Follow each of the installation steps. Make a list of each installation step, available installation options, and the option you selected. Include details about any unusual system behavior, error messages, or other messages that can be used for reference during future installations.
10. Review the new user help after installation has been completed.

UPGRADE CHECKLIST

1. Check system requirements by reading the Read1st.txt, Readme.doc, and any hardware compatibility information.
2. Determine whether your current operating system is supported for upgrade. Refer to Table 45.2.
3. Decide whether to upgrade any FAT or FAT32 partitions to NTFS (Windows NT/2000 only).
4. Review concepts for upgrading an existing domain if upgrading from an existing Windows NT domain (Windows 2000 Server only).
5. Review applications to be sure they are supported by the new operating system.
6. Back up files.
7. Remove/disable any current anti-virus software.
8. While the Windows 95/98 system is running, insert the upgrade CD-ROM into the CD drive.
9. Select the **Yes** option to begin the installation process. The Windows installation process will check the hard drive for errors.
10. Select **Next** to begin the installation.
11. Select the **I accept the license agreement** radio button and press the **Next** button.
12. Enter the **Windows Product Key** in the boxes provided and press the **Next** button.
13. Select **Yes** to save the existing system files.
14. Insert a floppy disk to create a startup disk and select the **OK** button.
15. Click **OK** when the Startup disk is complete to continue the setup operation.
16. Click **Finish** to begin copying the new operating system files. *Note:* This operation will take 30 minutes or more to complete depending on the speed of the computer system.
10. Make a note of each of the steps that are performed during the installation process.
11. Review the new user help information after the upgraded system is rebooted.

DISCUSSION AND CONCLUSION

Using a word processor, write your own detailed explanations of the results and observations made during the experiment. To begin, try to say something about each step.

In addition, provide answers to the following questions:

1. Why is it necessary to create an emergency disk?
2. Is it a good idea to save the current operation system files before performing an upgrade?
3. What are the advantages and disadvantages of performing an upgrade rather than a new installation?

Lab Activity 46
Adding/Removing
Windows Components

REFERENCE

Exercise 30

INTRODUCTION

In this lab activity, we examine the process of adding and removing Windows components.

PROCEDURE

TAKING INVENTORY OF THE INSTALLED COMPONENTS

1. Select the **Settings** option on the Start menu.
2. Select the **Control Panel**.
3. Double-click on the **Add/Remove Programs** icon to open the Add/Remove Programs Properties window as shown in Figure 46.1.
4. Click on the **Windows Setup** tab (or the **Add/Remove Windows Components** on Windows 2000).
5. Select the first component in the list.
6. Select the **Details** button to check the component features status. Make a note of each component and the features listed for each. *Note:* A blank check box indicates that no components are installed. A check box with a grey background with a check mark indicates that only some of the components are installed. A check box with a white background with a check mark indicates that all components are installed.
7. Repeat step 6 for the remaining components listed.
8. Left-click inside of the check box that contains a check mark and a white background and note the result.
9. Left-click inside of the check box again and note the result.
10. Left-click inside of the check box that contains a check mark and a gray background and note the result.
11. Left-click inside of the check box again and note the result.
12. Select a component category that is not completely installed (a check mark with a gray background).
13. Left-click on the **Details** button.
14. Left-click on a component that does not contain a check mark. Note the result.

FIGURE 46.1 Add/Remove Windows Components

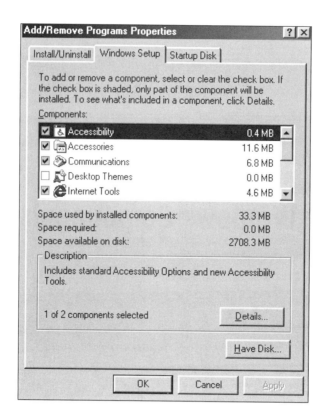

15. Left-click on a component that now contains a check mark. Note the result.
16. Scroll down the list of component items and identify which ones have additional details to review. Note their names.
17. Select **Cancel** to return to the Add/Remove Windows Components Properties window.
18. Select **Cancel** to close the Add/Remove Windows Components Properties window and cancel any additions or removals.
19. Select **OK** to close the Add/Remove Programs Properties window.

ADDING A COMPONENT

1. Double-click the **Add/Remove Programs** icon in the Control Panel.
2. Select the **Windows Setup** tab.
3. Locate a category that is not completely installed.
4. Left-click on the **Details** button.
5. Left-click on an empty check box to select the component for addition.
6. Note the amount of additional disk space required.
7. Click the **OK** button to return to the Add/Remove Programs Properties window.
8. Click **OK** to add the component.
9. Provide the Windows CD-ROM when requested.
10. Return to the Add/Remove Programs Properties window to see the result of the component addition.

REMOVING A WINDOWS COMPONENT

1. Double-click the **Add/Remove Programs** icon in the Control Panel.
2. Select the **Windows Setup** tab.
3. Locate a category that has at least one component installed.
4. Left-click on the **Details** button.

5. Left-click on an empty check box to select the component for removal.
6. Note the change in disk space required.
7. Click the **OK** button to return to the Add/Remove Programs Properties window.
8. Click **OK** to remove the component.
9. Return to the Add/Remove Programs Properties window to see the result of the component removal.

DISCUSSION AND CONCLUSION

Using a word processor, write your own detailed explanations of the results and observations made during the experiment. To begin, try to say something about each step.

In addition, provide answers to the following questions:

1. Is it a good idea to install all of the components?
2. Should the Games components be removed?
3. Compare the components on different versions of Windows.

Lab Activity 47
Installing/Removing Applications

REFERENCE

Exercises 30 and 35

INTRODUCTION

In this lab activity, we examine the steps required to install and remove applications in Windows.

PROCEDURE

TAKING INVENTORY OF THE INSTALLED PROGRAMS

1. Select the **Settings** option on the Start menu.
2. Select the **Control Panel**.
3. Double-click on the **Add/Remove Programs** icon to open the Add/Remove Programs Properties window as shown in Figure 47.1.
4. Make a note of all applications listed in the menu.
5. Examine the hard drive contents using Windows Explorer to identify corresponding installation directories.
6. Determine the amount of disk space used for each directory entry.
7. Close the Add/Remove Programs Properties window.

ADDING AN APPLICATION

1. Insert a CD-ROM containing a Windows application to be installed.
2. Follow all installation instructions, which typically include the following items:
   - Accept license agreements.
   - Supply a license key (on some application programs).
   - Determine a location on the hard drive to store application files.
   - Select a location in the Start menu for the application shortcut.
   - Specify any application-specific settings.
   - Register the application software.
3. Double-click the **Add/Remove Programs** icon in the Control Panel.

FIGURE 47.1 Add/Remove Programs Properties menu

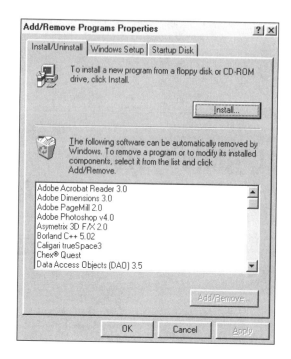

4. Locate the application in the list of installed applications.
5. Close the Add/Remove Program Properties window.
6. Locate the application files on the hard drive using Windows Explorer.
7. Locate the application shortcut file in the Start menu.
8. Determine the amount of disk space required.

REMOVING AN APPLICATION

1. Double-click the **Add/Remove Programs** icon in the Control Panel.
2. Locate the application to be removed in the list of installed programs.
3. Left-click on the **Add/Remove** button.
4. Select **Yes** to confirm the application program removal. Make a note of any messages displayed during the removal process.
5. Examine the hard drive using Windows Explorer to confirm the removal of all application files.
6. Examine the Start menu to verify the program shortcut has been removed.

DISCUSSION AND CONCLUSION

Using a word processor, write your own detailed explanations of the results and observations made during the experiment. To begin, try to say something about each step.

In addition, provide answers to the following questions:

1. Is it possible to identify the location on the hard drive for all applications listed on the Add/Remove Properties menu?
2. When a program is not listed on the Add/Remove Properties menu, how can the software be removed?
3. Why do some applications provide a link to the uninstallation program on the Start menu? Does this pose any problems?

Lab Activity 48
Security Techniques for the PC

REFERENCE

Exercise 38

INTRODUCTION

In this lab activity, we examine several aspects of system security. Each of the items should be evaluated to determine if the increased security would be worth the effort to implement them.

PROCEDURE

GENERAL WINDOWS SECURITY

1. Perform as many of the following security measures as possible:
   - Provide physical security for the computer system.
   - Use password security.
   - Password protect the screensaver.
   - Always run anti-virus software.
   - Perform regular backup procedures.
   - Secure all backup tapes.
   - Prevent the last logged-in user name from being displayed.
   - Check Microsoft's Web site for the latest updates.
   - Set a power-on BIOS password.
   - Disable the ability to boot from a floppy or CD-ROM on physically unsecured systems.
   - Use a firewall.
   - Implement IPSec protocol for IP traffic.
2. Add five additional items to the security measures list.

WINDOWS NT/2000 SECURITY

1. Perform as many of the following Windows 2000 security measures as possible:
   - Use the security configuration tools to configure policies.
   - Do not allow unmonitored modems in your environment.
   - Shut down unnecessary services and ports.
   - Enable auditing on system activity.

- Set permissions on the security event log.
- Store all sensitive documents on file servers.
- Disable the guest account.
- Limit the number of unnecessary accounts.
- Create two accounts for administrators.
- Use NTFS on all Windows NT/2000 partitions.
- Replace the "Everyone" group with "Authenticated Users" on file shares.

2. Add five additional security items to the Windows NT/2000 list.

DISCUSSION AND CONCLUSION

Using a word processor, write your own detailed explanations of the results and observations made during the experiment. To begin, try to say something about each step.

In addition, provide answers to the following questions:

1. Which of the items are the most important?
2. Which of the items are the least important?
3. What is the advantage of using NTFS when partitioning a disk using Windows NT/2000?

Lab Activity 49
Working with the Registry

REFERENCE

Exercise 27, Appendix K

INTRODUCTION

In this lab activity, we examine the system registry. *Note:* The system registry contains important setting and configuration information. If the registry is corrupted by user activity, the system can be rendered unbootable. Therefore, exercise extreme caution when working with the registry.

PROCEDURE

EXAMINE THE SYSTEM REGISTRY FILES

1. Open **Windows Explorer**.
2. Navigate to the **c:\windows** directory.
3. Select **Folder Options** from the View pull-down menu to display the Folder Options window as shown in Figure 49.1. *Note:* On Windows 2000 computer systems, Folder Options are located on the Tools pull-down menu.
4. Select **Folder Options** (or **Options** on Windows NT).
5. Verify that the **Show all files** option has been selected.
6. Look for the files SYSTEM.DAT and USER.DAT.
7. Record the file information (created date, modified date, access date, file size, etc.) from the properties window for each of the files.
8. Reboot the computer system.
9. Note the date and time for the files.

RUNNING THE REGISTRY EDITOR

1. Select the **Run** option on the Start menu.
2. Enter **Regedit** and press **Enter** to display the Registry Editor window shown in Figure 49.2.
3. Examine the name and the contents for each pull-down menu in the regedit window.
4. Study the contents of the regedit help menu.

FIGURE 49.1   Windows Folder Options

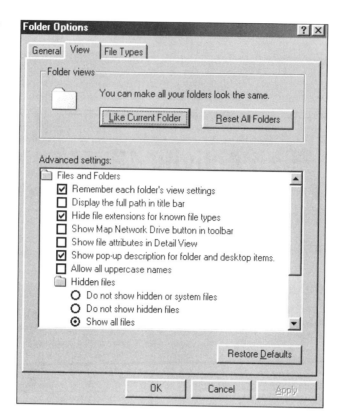

FIGURE 49.2   REGEDIT window

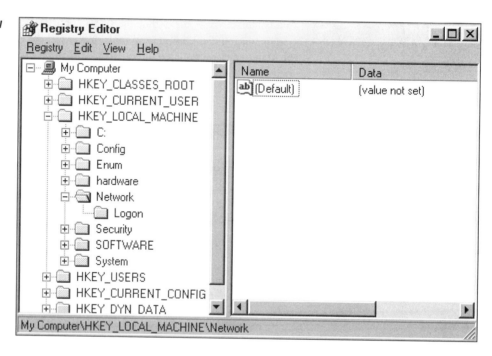

5. Note the number of entries and the entry names listed under the My Computer icon.

6. Select the first item in the list. Note the resulting change in the regedit display.

7. Left-click on the + (plus sign) inside of the box to the left of the first item in the list. Note the resulting change in the regedit display.

8. Left-click on and examine the settings for several of the items in the list.

9. Perform steps 7 and 8 for each of the remaining items listed on the regedit display.

10. Exit from the Registry editor.

EXPORTING THE REGISTRY

1. Open the **Registry Editor**.
2. Select the **My Computer** icon.
3. Select **Export Registry File** from the file pull-down menu.
4. Enter the name **allreg** in the file name field.
5. Repeat steps 3 and 4 for each the remaining items in the regedit menu and save them to disk. Select an appropriate name for each.
6. Note the size of each .reg file created.
7. Compare the size of the allreg.reg file to the size of the registry files you examined using Windows Explorer. State your findings.
8. Start the **Wordpad** accessory program.
9. Select **Open** from the File pull-down menu.
10. Select **All Documents (*.*)** from the Files of type text box.
11. Select **allreg.reg** from the list of available files and press the **Open** button.
12. Examine the contents of the allreg.reg file. Make a note of anything interesting.
13. Close the allreg.reg file.
14. Repeat steps 11 through 13 for all remaining exported registry files.

DISCUSSION AND CONCLUSION

Using a word processor, write your own detailed explanations of the results and observations made during the experiment. To begin, try to say something about each step.

In addition, provide answers to the following questions:

1. Why are the system registry files set to hidden and read only?
2. Can the system registry files be viewed from DOS?
3. What is the purpose of exporting registry entries?
4. Under what conditions would it be necessary to import a registry file?

Lab Activity 50
Troubleshooting Techniques

REFERENCE

All Exercises

INTRODUCTION

In this lab activity, we examine some troubleshooting techniques that may be useful. Each of the techniques listed is a recommendation that should be considered. Over a period of time, they may provide increased productivity, security, and satisfaction.

PROCEDURE

1. Examine the following list of techniques:
   - Always listen to problems and complaints.
   - Perform regular system backups.
   - Implement security relative to the importance of the activity.
   - Protect yourself and your customers from viruses.
   - Be cautious about sending unwanted e-mail.
   - Exercise extreme caution when working inside of a computer system.
   - Defragment a hard disk regularly to minimize time requirements.
   - Keep adequate printer supplies on hand.
   - Do not rush. Haste makes waste.
   - Never use harsh chemicals when maintaining computer equipment.
   - Use care when working with computer media.
   - Keep good records.
   - Always act in a professional manner.
   - Keep confidential customer information private.
   - Do not give up on a problem.
   - Compare prices on computer hardware and software to conserve money.
   - Invest in hardware and software tools that will increase your productivity.
   - Learn as much as possible about operating systems that you use.
   - Keep a detailed log of all problems and resolutions.
2. For hardware problems, consider these items:
   - Examine the interrupt, I/O port, and memory allocations for conflicts.
   - Verify that all adapter cards are seated properly.
   - Use Device Manager to check device status.
   - Check all cables for good connections, including internal cabling and external cabling.

3. Add your own hardware items to the list.
4. For software problems, keep these points in mind:
   - Is the problem an operating system problem or an application problem?
   - Has the software ever worked?
   - It is always acceptable to boot into Safe Mode. Sometimes problems fix themselves after a trip into Safe Mode.
   - Be patient. Sometimes a simple thing, like shutting down Windows, may take a long time.
   - Press **Ctrl-Alt-Del** if you think the system is hung. If the Close Program window comes up, that is a good sign that Windows is still running.
   - If Windows hangs up for a long time (for example, the mouse pointer does not move when you move the mouse), you may have to just turn the power off, reboot, and run SCANDISK to verify the integrity of your drives.
5. Add your own software tips to the list.
6. Review the Troubleshooting Techniques section at the end of each Exercise in *Mastering A+ Certification*. If required, add additional hardware and software techniques from the book to your lists in steps 1, 2, and 4.
7. Leave the room while your lab partner introduces an error into your lab computer. Then return and try to determine what the error is and how to repair it.

   The error introduced by your partner may be a software error or a hardware error. Your instructor may have you solve both kinds of errors. The nature of the error should be nondestructive. For example, do not cut one of the power cables going to the hard disk or delete an important system file.

   Instead, do something like the following:
   - Pull a USB or other connector partially out of its socket.
   - Change the interrupt of a hardware device.
   - Rename an important file, such as explorer.exe to explorer.tmp.
   - Hide files using ATTRIB.
   - Remove the system RAM or BIOS ROM.
   - Disconnect a power cable or signal cable to the floppy, hard disk, or CD-ROM.

DISCUSSION AND CONCLUSION

Using a word processor, write your own detailed explanations of the results and observations made during the experiment. To begin, try to say something about each step.

In addition, provide answers to the following questions:

1. What is the most important technique listed?
2. How do these troubleshooting techniques help to develop good computer habits?
3. What are the steps you took to solve the problem introduced by your lab partner?
4. How did you determine what error to introduce into the lab computer for your partner to solve?

NOTES

NOTES

NOTES

NOTES